Transplanted
to Better Health

4.16.13

Nancy,
   Be well! All the best!
Thanks for all that you did
for me.   Carole J. Favi

Transplanted

to Better Health

One woman's inspirational journey through
renal failure and dialysis to kidney transplant

Carole J. Fair

Fair Book Publishing
1522 Collingdale Circle
Mechanicsburg, PA 17050-7319

This book is the story of one person's experience with kidney transplant. It is not intended as a reference volume or a medical manual, and it is not a substitute for medical diagnosis. If you suspect that you have a medical problem, we urge you to seek competent medical help. Mention of specific hospitals, organizations or authorities in this book does not imply endorsement by the author, nor does mention of specific hospitals, organizations or authorities imply that they endorse this book or its author.

Internet addresses and telephone numbers given in this book were accurate at the time it went to press.

ISBN-13: 978-1475224832
ISBN-10: 1475224834

*In loving memory of
my parents and sister*

Table of Contents

Prologue

FLIGHT 227 FROM Pittsburgh to Harrisburg carried a very special passenger on Monday, February 21, 2011. In an exclusive seat all its own was the plastic picnic container that housed my new kidney. It came from the Thomas E. Starzl Transplant Institute of the University of Pittsburgh Medical Center. I will always remember that President's Day, for it was the day I was scheduled to have my kidney transplant surgery. At Harrisburg Hospital, the medical staff began hustling, as I was not quite ready for the Operating Room (OR). The anesthesiologist came in to talk with me, an IV was started, and down the hall I went on my grey, steel gurney to the OR. There, I would await my new kidney, arriving via courier service from the airport.

I was really rather nervous. I asked to be given something to take the edge off things, and when I was, that was all I remembered... until I woke up in the Recovery Room (RR). Here, the new kidney worked just beautifully, pouring out its golden liquid. I was told I kept complaining, "I'm cold, I'm cold!" My head was totally wrapped in a towel, and all that was visible were my eyes and nose. The nurses poured fluids into me through my IV, but the new kidney seemed to get ahead of them. I later learned that sometimes when a new kidney is placed into the recipient, it simply goes flat and doesn't kick off right away. What an unsettling problem that would be! I was so grateful my new kidney began working immediately.

And now, my second chance at life began...

CHAPTER 1

About Me

IF YOU ARE reading my story, perhaps you are nervously awaiting a new kidney like I was. Or maybe your spouse is on the waiting list and you're along for the journey. As a patient, I never quite understood the whole picture, as I was just taken through the process step by step. Seeing the entire picture and understanding the complete process will only enhance your end result. For the past four years as I traveled the road to receiving my new kidney, I have kept a personal journal. I have walked the walk, and now I'm able to talk the talk with both empathy and essential facts. Let me tell you a little bit about myself so that you will understand my life until kidney disease changed it.

When a baby is born, most parents look for ten fingers and ten toes. Who thinks to look for a perfect kidney in their newborn? Well, I wish the doctors had. I was born on May 8, 1944, at St. Luke's Hospital in Bethlehem, PA.

I was a seemingly healthy baby, 6 pounds, 13 ounces, and 19 inches long. My parents were John and Julie Pipok, and I had a sister, Eleanor Elaine, who was ten years older. I grew up in a very close-knit, loving, and nurturing family.

As a young child, I often had sore throats, even some streptococcal infections. The doctor suggested I get my tonsils out before I started kindergarten. At the age of five, I had them removed, and this seemed to eliminate the sore throat problem. I often wondered, however, if these strep infections may have caused some of my kidney damage. I later learned that certain strains of strep are more damaging than others to kidney membranes.

Shortly after I graduated from college, I was admitted to Harrisburg Hospital to have all four of my wisdom teeth removed. A routine urinalysis revealed protein in my urine, not at all normal. Later that year, I was admitted to the hospital by an urologist for tests to rule out kidney disease. At first, tuberculosis of the kidneys was suspected, but that test proved negative. Other tests and x-rays followed until I was finally diagnosed with reflux disease, a congenital problem. Apparently, this was the cause of my pyelonephritis (kidney infections) and, eventually, my chronic renal insufficiency.

Reflux is a birth defect in which the sphincter muscle doesn't work properly. The urine normally flows from the kidneys through the ureters to the bladder and out of the body. Normally, there is a valve (sphincter) that prevents the urine from going from the bladder back into the ureter, but my sphincter muscle didn't work properly and the urine would back-up into the ureters and the kidneys. This "reflux of the urine from the bladder" caused scarring and damage to the kidneys. In the 1940s, sphincter muscle surgery had to be done by age five to be successful, and even then, the success rate was only 50%. (I learned that when I was 21 years old.) My particular kidney disease was a very insidious problem, slowly creeping up on me over time and with all its ugly symptoms.

I graduated from the Harrisburg Institute of Medical Arts in Harrisburg, PA, in 1964. It was a two-year course through both summers. Upon graduation, I became employed as a medical technician, and several years later, I became certified as a medical assistant. My career in medicine was quite varied and included managing a cardiologist's office, working in a hospital laboratory and a private laboratory, and working for a medical malpractice insurance company that insured both hospitals and physicians. Later, this medical background would help me understand my kidney problem better and become an active participant with my doctors to improve my health. In other words, it would enable me to become an empowered patient.

I married rather late in life, having had a number of sad relationships, including the death of my fiancé, an Air Force captain who was killed in the Vietnam War. I was so happy when I met Don and we began dating. He asked my father for my hand in marriage just one week before Dad died. After our wedding on October 15, 1983, I moved into Don's home in King of Prussia, PA. Eight months later, he had a job transfer to Mechanicsburg, PA, where we have lived for the past 27 years.

Don and I also have a home in Bethlehem, my hometown. After my parents passed away, we decided to keep the house, did some remodeling, and now come here monthly for long weekends. I love this getaway home — it's filled with so many wonderful memories and great times. My father, John, was a carpenter for the Bethlehem Steel Company for more than 45 years. He built this brick Cape Cod house and it was here where my sister and I were raised. My dear mother, Julie, was a very loving woman and a wonderful cook. My childhood was simple, but quite happy.

I had always wanted children, but was told by my doctor that I should not become pregnant. My damaged kidneys would need to filter for both the baby and me, so pregnancy and childbirth were too risky. I was devastated by this news. Don and I talked about it at great length. In lieu of having our own children, we decided to become foster parents with Cumberland County Children & Youth Services. Chad, a 5-year-old boy, came to live with us, and we were the fifth set of foster parents for this child. He had many challenges. We worked with him daily for about a year until his case went to court. The judge declared the natural mother fit and able to care for him, so he was removed from our care. The way I saw it, this could not have been further from the truth. When I lost Chad to what I considered an unfit mother still on drugs, I was very discouraged with the legal system and simply chose not to continue to foster any more children.

Don has two children — a daughter, Leslie, and a son, Gregg — from a previous marriage. They were now both teenagers. We thought one of the local foreign exchange programs might be a better fit for us.

We applied, and over the years, enjoyed having three foreign exchange "daughters" live with us. Marta was from Barcelona, Spain; Vivi was from Hamburg, Germany; and Claudia was from Recife, Brazil. Claudia spent an entire year with us, enjoying her senior year in an American high school, and it was such a positive experience for all of us. A few years after she returned home, we visited her and her family in Brazil. Such fun! To this day, we continue to maintain contact with her, now a professional chef and restaurant owner, married, and the mother of a two-year-old son.

All my life I had wanted a dog. As a child, my father was allergic to the one and only pet I ever had, a white rabbit named Pete. Now that I was married and had time to care for a pet, I decided to buy a dog. After researching a number of library books on dog breeds, Don and I fell in love with a picture of a Cavalier King Charles Spaniel. That was the dog for us! We found a breeder and bought our Brandie, and she became a wonderful companion to us. Since her father was a champion, we trained her for the show ring, and we also trained her in agility and in obedience. A smart and playful puppy, she was only 11 weeks old when we brought her home. This affectionate little dog added so much to our lives.

After my mother passed away in May 1997, I decided to start my own home business. I always had a keen business sense and an entrepreneurial spirit. However, I had no idea what I could do. When I visited a friend who had recently started her own embroidery and monogramming business, I became enthralled with all the pretty thread colors on her rack. I love color! As a child, I remember coloring for hours in my coloring books.

When I was young, my mother taught me to embroider by hand, and I enjoyed doing that. But this was computerized embroidery and it was totally different. Nevertheless, I decided this was the business for me. I could actually do this. My niche became a fabric gift shop of sorts, and "Amazing Monograms" was born. I sold items for all members of the family and for those special milestones in their lives. In this cottage industry, I purchased quality items from about 19 wholesalers throughout the United States. I embellished these items by either monogramming or embroidering our very own designs on them. If someone wanted a special and unique gift, I believed I had it.

I worked very hard the first three years trying to get this business up and running. I loved doing what I was doing and it fueled my days. In 2000, Don joined me as a digitizer, and the business really took off. He took classes to be able to do the embroidery art work and became quite proficient. With his ability to put logos on shirts and caps, he added another dimension to our business. We now have a solid, loyal customer base that visits my shop frequently to buy their gifts. Mostly though, we advertise at craft shows where finished products can be purchased right from our table.

In the fall of 2009, Don and I talked about stretching our monogramming business a little. We had been in business for 13 years, and I just felt we needed something more. Short-story version, in January 2010, we decided to purchase an alpaca! We would use her wonderful, soft-like-cashmere fleece to make unique items to sell in our shop.

We bought Brynia, a pregnant white female who was due to deliver her cria (baby alpaca) in July 2010. It was truly an emotional business decision and probably the first time in my life I had done so little research before jumping in with both feet. We decided to board the animals at the farm where we had purchased them. What an adventure this was going to be! I wanted something that I knew nothing about, so I could expand my thinking and network with new people, and I loved animals. I wanted something, too, that would boost my spirits and give me a reason to wake up excited each morning, and owning alpacas seemed to fit that criteria well.

On July 12, 2010, Brynia gave birth to a light-fawn male, whom my husband lovingly named Apollo 18. He was just too cute for words. We chose to show Apollo the following spring, and I planned to train him after he was weaned from his mother to get him ready for the show ring. It was to be such a fun time for us.

I was feeling okay at this point in time, not yet symptomatic, but I sensed my time as a healthy woman was running short and that I would soon experience difficulties with my kidney disease.

In late January 2011, in the midst of my health problems, Brandie became very ill. She had an enlarged heart, common to this breed, and suffered from breathing difficulties. She refused to eat for four days and I couldn't get her to take any of her heart medications. Brandie truly lived to eat! I had always thought that a true sign that she had given up would be when she stopped eating. We took her to the vet on January 24 and had her put down. It nearly broke our hearts. Brandie was 15 years old. She had lived much longer than we had ever thought she would. Nonetheless, it was a sadness I hadn't expected to experience at that time. Don built a wooden coffin for her and we held a funeral service full of prayers and love that would bring anyone to tears.

Proudly, Don and I are grandparents. We have four wonderful grandchildren — the twins, Megan and Michael, now in their third year at the University of Delaware; Cheyenne, age 8; and Grayson, age 5. What a great extension of life! They bring so much joy to us, and we look forward to their visits, especially the adventurous summer stays with the younger ones.

I have always enjoyed talking to people in a teaching capacity. Serving as a volunteer docent for the Pennsylvania Governor's Residence for the past ten years has been most enjoyable for me. Along with a staff of 45 other docents, I have toured countless guests through the home, providing them with historical details of the residence and information on the current art display. I also serve as a tour guide with Hershey Entertainment and Resort Company. I board the chartered buses that come into Hershey, PA, telling the tourists the life story of Milton Hershey, how he developed the school for disadvantaged children, and how he built the town of Hershey around his most beloved chocolate factory.

That was my life up to this point, a very good life basically. And I was grateful for all of it…the ups and even the downs. Spending time with God was the high-light of my days and proved to be the foundation for my life. I relied on my devout faith and trust in Him to see me through the difficult times and my good common sense to get me through the day-to-day trials. Common sense, which is not so common nowadays, had always served me well.

I was about to experience a most challenging time with my health. It would prove to be a very humbling and difficult experience for me. Never could I have imagined what lay ahead...

CHAPTER 2

The National Kidney Transplant List

Maybe you anticipate being on the National Kidney Transplant List, or are already are on it. What is it exactly? How does it work? And what are the requirements to get listed? These were my questions, too.

The National Kidney Transplant List actually works on a point system and is a rather complicated process. Points are assigned patients based on their time on the list, their genetic match with a potential donor, and the antibody level of the recipient. Pediatric patients receive additional points. I learned that the best match is when the tissues of both donor and recipient are a six-antigen match. The only perfect match is from an identical twin, although rare cases of rejection have been reported. While on the list, it would be important for me to stay as healthy as possible, to exercise and stay active, to follow my diet, not to skip dialysis treatments (if I were on dialysis), and to get labs drawn regularly.

The United Network for Organ Sharing (UNOS) was established in 1977 and is responsible for sharing organs. National criteria was developed for placement on the transplant list. When a patient is approved for a transplant following a transplant evaluation, their medical information is entered into the UNOS database. This information includes the recipient's blood type, HLA (or genetic markers), the date they started dialysis, and other laboratory data. When a potential donor is identified, much of the same information is also entered into the database. The computer system checks the list frequently and potential recipients are identified. If a kidney is donated in a given area, it will be offered first in that area, then regionally, and finally, at the national level.

Throughout most my life, I doctored with a number of kidney specialists. For the past seven years, however, Jonathan R. Diamond, MD, was my nephrologist. He followed my health with office visits and blood tests every six months. My blood tests now revealed kidneys that were slowly deteriorating and becoming dangerously low functioning. I was beginning to experience end-stage renal disease (ESRD).

Twenty million Americans of all ages have chronic kidney disease and another 20 million Americans are at risk for developing kidney disease. Diabetes, high blood pressure, and polycystic kidney disease are three major causes of chronic kidney disease. I first experienced high blood pressure about 15 years ago, long after my problem originated. Fortunately for me, I don't have diabetes. High blood sugars (diabetes type 1 and diabetes type 2) can overwork the kidneys, causing them to stop functioning adequately. With an early diagnosis, kidney disease can be slowed with treatment, but with a later diagnosis, kidney failure usually results.

Kidneys are truly remarkable organs. Inside them are millions of tiny blood vessels that act as filters, removing toxins and waste products from the blood. They also produce hormones that help to regulate blood pressure and red blood cell production. Finally, kidneys help balance and control (get rid of or keep) fluid in the body, as well as maintain salt and acid levels. Kidneys with normal function are able to perform all of these activities without difficulty. Kidneys that are damaged are unable to perform some or all of these jobs. This can lead to build-up of excess fluid, waste products, high blood pressure, and a low blood count. When this occurs, dialysis and medications are needed to clear these waste products and prevent death.

Dr. Diamond wanted me to observe a low-protein, low-salt diet, which I did for about five years. He felt that doing this would delay the demise of my kidneys, as protein is hard for the kidneys to break down. Such a diet is difficult to follow, as there is protein in almost all foods. But I tried and was very conscientious about it.

During an office visit in the summer of 2007, Dr. Diamond suggested I consider placement on the National Kidney Transplant List. He believed that although I might not need a new kidney for awhile, being on the list would at least start the clock ticking. Currently, there are more than 100,000 people waiting for a kidney transplant in the United States. Dr. Diamond felt he would be remiss as a physician if he didn't suggest this to me then because there was a 4 to 6 year wait for a cadaver kidney. I had no suitable living relatives, so this would probably be the way I would go.

Feeling just fine, I was shocked by all this. I left Dr. Diamond's office in a daze and went home to digest the news. I had always thought I would be on dialysis for a number of years before a transplant would even be considered. However, I wasn't on dialysis yet, and Dr. Diamond was talking transplant. I was in total disbelief. And what if I didn't receive a new kidney? Would I experience life-long dialysis, or maybe even death? I knew so little, and many questions needed to be answered.

This is where faith came in. My mother was very religious, and I had gone to church my entire life and truly believed in God and His mercy. My religion is Russian Orthodox. Over the years I had developed a wonderful personal relationship with God, which was so important to me. I talk with Him daily and count on His guidance. My faith is strong, but having faith in God doesn't mean just sitting back and doing nothing. I knew God would help me when He saw that I was actively trying to help myself. I needed to do my part. I also trusted God that I was exactly where I was meant to be. All in all, I just couldn't imagine getting through something like this without a very strong belief system.

September 24, 2007

And now my journey begins. Don and I attend an all-day meeting at Harrisburg Hospital. It is primarily for educational purposes. We watch a film on what to expect with dialysis and listen to the nurse explain transplantation. I look around at the people in attendance, mostly couples, and I honestly can't tell which one is the patient and which one accompanied them. They all look relatively healthy, especially for being at such a session. It always amazed me to learn who the patient actually was; I usually guessed wrong.

We meet with Jeri Goldman, RN, CCTC, Pre-Transplant Coordinator, and I find her to be really upbeat and friendly. She puts me at ease immediately and I'm very comfortable talking to her. Jeri takes detailed medical and social histories and just asks me a lot of questions in general. She questions whether or not I have a Living Will. Actually, I have a Living Trust in place. Jeri tells me that she will be responsible for walking me through the entire transplant process.

We then meet Harold C. Yang, MD, PhD, Medical Director of the PinnacleHealth Transplant Program/Attending Surgeon, Central Pennsylvania Transplant Associates. Don and I are in awe. When we're introduced to him, we both respectfully stand up. I just can't imagine a doctor trained to do transplant surgeries. Truly remarkable!

I know the medical personnel here at Harrisburg Hospital are all well-trained and extremely competent, but they are also strangers who I have no relationship with. It makes me a little apprehensive. I suppose, though, with time this will all change as they get to know me and I become more comfortable with them.

November 26, 2007

In order to qualify for the National Kidney Transplant List, I need to have a number of routine diagnostic tests done. Earlier this year, I had a colonoscopy with good results. Now, a Thallium Stress Test, a PPD test (for tuberculosis), a chest x-ray (to identify any abnormalities of my lungs and respiratory tract), a blood draw for many lab tests, and a pneumococcal vaccine are all scheduled at Harrisburg Hospital. It weighs heavily on my mind.

I wish I didn't have to get the vaccine — I never even had a flu shot. I try hard to feel well, look well, and be well, and now I'm scheduled to have all these things done to me, and I begin to feel sick. If you have felt well most of your life and then become seriously ill, it's a lot more difficult to handle than if you had experienced health problems throughout your life. That was my situation. I never really had a major health problem before, so it was not an easy time for me.

November 27, 2007

This turns out to be an exhausting day. Nuclear Medicine is a real experience — from claustrophobic patients in the "picture machine" to a Code Blue being called in the elevator. I was trying to get back to the department on a timed test, but I found the elevator going in the opposite direction because of the code. I was sure I was going to be late for my final pictures. Well, I made it, and it seems as if the timing was not all that critical after all. Then, following the completion of my last cardiac pictures, the fire alarm goes off. I find myself walking down four flights of steps, as I'm just not going to take any chances with the elevator again. Other people have the same idea.

I have all the tests done, and I'm so glad when the day is finally over. I'm tired of worrying about these tests.

Now, in retrospect, these tests were just the beginning and the very least of my worries.

During a phone conversation, Jeri informed me that I now had to have a letter from my dentist, indicating my teeth were in good condition. A dental exam would detect infections, cavities, or gum disease, which could be a source of infection after transplant. I also had to have a mammography, pelvic examination, and Pap test with negative results. So I went ahead and made the appointments with the appropriate doctors. The results needed to be in as soon as possible and, hopefully, I would then qualify for the National Kidney Transplant List. It seemed to me you needed to be in good health to be considered, in spite of your kidney problem. Actually I was in fairly good health and would probably make a good transplant candidate. I didn't have diabetes or a heart condition, and I was not overweight.

Jeri mentioned that the statistics were just in on successful transplants at one year post-surgery at Harrisburg Hospital. The hospital had a 98% success rate. It seems that post-transplant care is extremely important and the staff gives concentrated care to each patient. Since starting the program in 2000, PinnacleHealth Transplant Services has performed more than 750 kidney and kidney/pancreas transplants. I saw that as definite confirmation that I was at the right hospital and with the right doctors for my transplant. I was advised that I could multilist with other transplant centers as well, but I didn't consider that an option for me.

I was told that after my pre-transplant evaluation was completed and the results were in, the information would be discussed by the Selection Committee. They would meet to review my data, and my potential candidacy for transplantation would be determined. The committee consisted of the transplant surgeons, nephrologists, transplant coordinators (both pre- and post-), research transplant coordinators, transplant social workers, transplant financial counselors, living donor coordinators, and support staff. Quite a team!

December 6, 2007
I receive a congratulatory letter in the mail. It reads that my pre-transplant evaluation has been completed, and that as of November 30, 2007, I became actively enrolled on the National Kidney Transplant List. How wonderful is that! This will be a date I will long remember. It seems to me that only a "healthy" patient gets on this list.

Now that I was listed, I was required to get my blood drawn the first week of every month. This blood sample would be used to do an antibody screening (PRA), as well as to test my blood against blood samples of potential donors in an effort to find a match. I had blood drawn faithfully every month for more than three years. Not to have done so would have delayed or postponed my transplant.

I learned that transplantation actually started in the 1950s, and the most effective immunosuppressant drugs became available in the 1980s — all fairly recently, really. It's absolutely amazing to me. Medicine certainly has come a long way in treating kidney disease. How lucky for me that if I had to have a kidney problem, it was now. Having kidney disease need not be a death sentence, but in order to manage it successfully, I must be a very compliant patient.

March 20, 2008

I have an appointment with Dr. Diamond today. He informs me that I am now "On Hold — Status 7" on the National Kidney Transplant List. This means that time will accrue, but I will not be called for a transplant. I have few symptoms and I'm really feeling okay. My glomerular filtration rate (GFR), which indicates how well my kidneys are filtering, is 19.8%, slightly under the 20% maximum percentage allowed to qualify for listing.

October 1, 2008

Today, Don and I attend our first Central Pennsylvania Coalition for Transplantation support group meeting at a local hospital. Dr. Yang speaks, and there are a good many people present. Apparently, a number of governmental changes are about to take place. Beginning in 2009, the government may have a say as to who gets a kidney and who doesn't. Several factors will be considered including age, weight, and whether or not the patient has diabetes or a cardiac condition. Age worries me. Perhaps when I'm ready, I'll be too old to qualify. It's really a little scary, but I place this all in God's hands. He's in control and already knows the end result. I put my inner dialogue to rest and simply focus on what lies immediately ahead of me.

CHAPTER 3

Types of Transplants

KIDNEY TRANSPLANTS ARE second only to corneal transplants as the most common transplant operation in the United States. There are over 9,000 kidney transplants performed each year.

There are basically two types of kidney transplants — a deceased donor transplant and a living donor transplant. A deceased donor transplant occurs when someone has been determined brain dead (no brain activity) or when someone has experienced an irreversible brain injury and the family decides to withdraw life support (donation after cardiac death). A living donor transplant occurs when a living person volunteers to donate one of their kidneys to another person in need.

There are several types of living donor transplants:

1. **Living Related** — A kidney is donated from someone who is genetically related to the recipient.
2. **Living Unrelated** — A kidney is donated from some-

one who is known to the recipient (friend, co-worker, etc.), but there is no genetic relationship.

3. **Good Samaritan** — A kidney is donated from someone who feels emotionally or socially drawn to help another in need and is a stranger to the recipient.

4. **Paired Exchange** — A paired exchange transplant occurs when incompatible living donors and recipient pairs exchange (or swap) donor kidneys with another incompatible pair. This allows both patients to receive a living donor transplant and the benefits that go along with a living donor transplant.

I wonder which of these, if any, will become my saving grace.

CHAPTER 4

The Paired Donor List

Medicine is constantly advancing and this is certainly true in the specialty of kidney disease. The Paired Donor List is an excellent example of moving forward.

January 16, 2009

Today, a letter arrives from PinnacleHealth Transplantation Services of Harrisburg Hospital. They have just partnered with the Paired Donor Network. According to Dr. Yang, "This partnership has tremendous flexibility for the donor and recipient, and several quality transplant programs in the country are participating in this new program, e.g., UCLA and Emory. We are very excited about this development, as it has the potential to get many of our patients transplanted." Encouraging, indeed! I know that should I ever find someone willing to donate their kidney to me and we aren't a match, the Paired Donor List would certainly be my next step.

March 17, 2009

Today, a very important meeting is scheduled at Harrisburg Hospital to discuss the Paired Donor List. Don and I decide to go, but when we arrive, there is no one there. I can't figure this out, so when we get home, I check the calendar and, sure enough, the meeting is on our calendar for today. I call Transplant Services the next day, and I learn that the meeting was held on Tuesday, February 17. I had marked it on the wrong month on my calendar. To make it even more confusing, the date happens to be the same day for both months. How disappointing!

Jeri explained the new program to us, but I wished Don and I had heard it firsthand at the meeting and in more detail. Briefly, if you knew someone who wanted to donate their kidney to you, but you weren't a match, you could be placed on the Paired Donor List. It gives you the possibility of being matched with a donor in another area of the state or region. Donors are truly American heroes, no matter where they live.

On November 11, 2010, Katie Couric had interviewed Garet and Jan Hil for CBS News. Three years ago, this couple watched their life unravel when their 10-year-old daughter, Samantha, experienced complete kidney failure brought on by a rare genetic disease. "Before this diagnosis," Couric asked Garet, "you knew nothing about kidney failure?" Garet commented, "I didn't even know I had two kidneys before this — it was, you know, not on the radar." After many obstacles, Samantha's 23-year-old cousin proved to be a match, and Samantha was transplanted successfully.

Garet was CEO of a software company when he helped launched the National Kidney Registry. He knew of the difficulties he and his wife had encountered prior to Samantha's match, and he wanted to simplify this process for others. To date, this database holds nearly 100,000 records of people who need kidneys and their loved ones who are willing to give up one of theirs to anyone who promises to keep the donor chain going. Currently, 50 centers across the country are enrolled in this program. The largest recorded chain involved 28 lives at the Methodist San Antonio Transplant Center in San Antonio, TX. "The bigger the swap you can get, the more people can get transplanted faster," said Garet.

CHAPTER 5

The Road Is Long

Perhaps you are traveling now on that bumpy road of chronic illness. Maybe you're experiencing the ups and downs of kidney disease, but are still remaining optimistic that better health will return...somehow and somewhere in the future. It's a discouraging time indeed. Here is how I remember my darkest days.

October 22, 2008

I have an appointment with Dr. Diamond today. My lab tests did not yield good results. My creatinine is now up to 3 mg/dL. A normal result is between 0.5 to 1.5 mg/ dL. Creatinine are colorless crystals and are one of the non-protein constituents of blood and urine — a true picture of kidney function. Increased quantities of creatinine are found in advanced renal disease.

I have no symptoms other than occasional shortness of breath. An EKG and an echocardiogram are ordered to check this out and an appointment is made with a pulmonologist.

The cardiac tests were both fine. I saw the pulmonologist and the breathing tests were normal, too. It was determined that I may have mild asthma, but I decided against taking any medication at this time. My shortness of breath didn't happen often and I was simply relieved to know it wasn't my heart.

November 3, 2008
Dr. Diamond wants me to have a chest x-ray. I'll have this done along with my monthly blood draw.

It was normal.

This week, my toes, feet and ankles begin to swell. I have a bad feeling. Maybe I just need a diuretic, like Lasix. Will that help? I certainly hope so.

December 19, 2008
Today, I begin Lasix, 20 mg every other day. It works, but this can't be a good sign. If I need medication to remove fluid, it means my kidneys are not able to and need some help.

The week of January 26, 2009, finds me suffering from screaming right big toe and foot pain. I have never experienced anything like this before. When I try to sleep at night, just having the top sheet cover my foot is so awfully painful I can barely stand it. I call Dr. Diamond and he prescribes a dose of prednisone. I now have gout, he says, a side effect of failing kidneys.

I schedule a DEXA scan appointment for February 2, 2009, so when I have my monthly blood draw, I'll also be tested for osteoporosis. It has been two years since my last DEXA scan, which is the minimum time needed between scans for my insurance company to pay, and I'm anxious to have it done to compare results.

It revealed that I now have osteopenia, not quite as serious as osteoporosis, but I'm on my way.

February 4, 2009

I go to this month's support group meeting and listen to an endocrinologist speak. She discusses nutrition, food portions, etc., for renal and diabetic patients. I learn that I might become "temporarily" diabetic immediately after the transplant, but hopefully, my blood sugars will return to normal as my prednisone dose is lowered. In fact, I will be given IV insulin in the hospital just before the surgery. I learn lots of frightening things, many of which I think I'd be better off not knowing. Sometimes life gets too complicated to figure it all out on your own. When that happens, I let God do the figuring. I just need to do the next thing and not borrow any problems from tomorrow.

I finish the prednisone for gout in my foot. It finally resolves, and I can now walk and do my exercises again. I work out at the gym about 2 to 3 times a week. I begin taking two medications that will help prevent further episodes of gout — allopurinol and colchicine. Having gout is truly having excruciating pain and I hope never to experience that again.

May 14, 2009

I'm not looking forward to this visit with Dr. Diamond. I know my blood tests will not be good. And the fact that I have had gout, kidney-related, since I last saw him is definitely not a good sign. My visit is rather rushed, but I'm sure Dr. Diamond has much on his mind. I complain again of shortness of breath, so he puts me on Singulair. I hope this helps.

Well, I was right. My GFR is down to 15.5 (from 19.9) with an increase in creatinine to 3.2 mg/dL (from 3). My phosphorus went up, although I'm not being treated for that yet. Maybe that's why my fingers and toes are cramping up.

I'm starting to worry more. I try to let go and let God, but it's not always easy to do. This should be more than just a slogan, it should become a way of life, and I need to make it a definite way of thinking in my life.

I have concerns about my business. How am I to plan for the future of my embroidery gift shop? Should I order more items or sell out what I have? I usually sign up for craft shows six months in advance and they are expensive. Will I be well enough to attend these shows, or will I lose the money I have spent on my space? Don and I also talk about going to Germany next year for a vacation, as he wants to do some genealogy work there. I doubt that I'll be able to make such a trip. I know my health will fail, but I just don't know when. Then again, I guess none of us do… Lots to think about, and it's really mind boggling. I guess I just need to place my life on hold.

May 27, 2009

I'm having problems with indigestion. I remember Dr. Diamond asking me if I was having this as a symptom. It's almost every day now, and when it happens, I have no appetite.

June 8, 2009

I receive a call from Madeline Sica, RN, BSN, at Transplant Services. She introduces herself and tells me Jeri is in charge of living donors, so she is now my pre-transplant coordinator.

July 21, 2009

I see my gynecologist (OB/GYN) today, since I have been having a lot of hot flashes and, even worse, night sweats. I don't know why. I went off hormones a few years back and had these problems for the next three years, but then they went away. Now they're back and I don't think it's normal. She wants to call Dr. Diamond, as it may be kidney related (a problem with my immune system), and then she'll get back to me. It seems as if everything is related to my kidneys. If it weren't for my sick kidneys, I'd be a totally healthy person. Instead, I have ailments galore.

August 14, 2009

I learn today that the thyroid and hormone tests ordered by my OB/GYN are okay, although my parathyroid test is slightly elevated. Now what does that mean?

August 16, 2009

I'm getting dressed for church when I look in the mirror to put my makeup on and see how very pale I am. I bet my hemoglobin and hematocrit (H & H) are low. At the same time, I realize I don't feel well — my heart rate is up and I feel nauseous. So much so that I just can't go to church today. I'm afraid I'll pass out. I check my calendar and realize I'm overdue to take Kionex, a medication that helps to flush the potassium out of my body since my kidneys can no longer do this. If my potassium gets too high, it can affect my heart. And Dr. Diamond is on vacation this week. I take it, as my last dose was four days ago instead of three days between doses. I begin to feel a little better, probably just another problem that will pass.

September 1, 2009

Today, I have my three-month appointment with Dr. Diamond. I ask Don to come along with me for support. It will be the first time Don meets Dr. Diamond. I have been seeing him for seven years, since 2003, but I have always gone to my appointments alone.

I stress to Dr. Diamond that I have been having night sweats for about three months. He orders three tests — a CT scan, a chest x-ray, and a test for tuberculosis.

September 3, 2009

A CT scan is performed today. I have never had one before. Quite an amazing machine! And fortunately, my head doesn't have to go all the way in. This would become a problem for me because I'm claustrophobic. I'm hoping they don't find anything. That's all I need in addition to my failing kidneys — another major problem, like cancer.

Fortunately, all three tests that Dr. Diamond ordered were negative.

February 22, 2010

I have an appointment for an esophagogastroduodenoscopy (EGD) and a routine colonoscopy today. I'm having problems with indigestion and belching.

Well, everything turned out okay. Biopsies were taken for colitis and celiac disease, and both came back negative. I still didn't feel well. Could it be my kidneys? The doctor wanted to do one more test. The cost was $2,000, but the nurse in his office said that Medicare won't pay for it. This test would check the section of bowel that the doctor couldn't reach. The nurse strongly suggested that I have it done; however, I wanted to await the results of my blood tests. My blood will be drawn tomorrow. If the kidneys haven't gotten any worse and aren't causing these problems, then I'll go ahead with the test. I'm tired of being nauseated all the time.

March 4, 2010

Dr. Diamond places me on Prilosec and I decide not to have this expensive test done.

March 16, 2010

Another checkup with Dr. Diamond. I don't expect much to change, but it has. My creatinine has gone up again and is now 3.3 mg/dL. Maybe I need to drink more water. I was told to drink nine glasses daily and for most days, I do. Sometimes, though, I simply forget to count the glasses. I tell Dr. Diamond that my pulse seems high, and I can feel it racing almost every day.

Midway through the night tonight, I awake and experience a metal taste in my mouth. Truthfully speaking, this is probably the third time it has happened and each time it was during the night. It does go away quickly though. I'm afraid to say something to Dr. Diamond because I know this is not good. I later learn that this symptom appears when the urea increases to a point where only dialysis can remove it.

March 17, 2010

*My pulse is 120 beats per minute this morning. I have a hairdresser's appointment, and I feel just blah and have no appetite. Last evening when I awoke in the middle of the night, I had a severe headache and vomited twice. There was hardly anything in my stomach as I hadn't eaten much that day. Is **this** the beginning of kidney failure?*

March 18, 2010

I awake and feel just great. Now, can you believe this? It is unbelievable. Like night and day. I call Dr. Diamond's office, and his nurse tells me to monitor these episodes.

I think I'm probably right on the cusp between no dialysis and dialysis. I'm drinking nine glasses of water faithfully every day to flush my kidneys. I hope to never feel as sick as I did yesterday.

April 20, 2010

Something is very wrong, and I think it may be that my hemoglobin and hematocrit are low. My heart is almost always pounding, and my pulse is up between 96 and 120 beats per minute. I'm sleeping ten hours every night and about every other day, I also need a nap. This is not me.

I have an appointment with Dr. Diamond today, and it can't come soon enough. Dr. Diamond wants more blood tests — he isn't sure if my H&H are low because of iron-deficiency anemia or because of kidney disease. Also, he is looking at March 1 lab work, and that's a bit out of date. He wants to see current test results. I want to know, too, so I'll have my blood drawn later today to get some answers.

April 21, 2010

Results are in, and my hemoglobin is 10.6 g (normal is 11 -18 g) and my hematocrit is 32% (normal is 35 to 54%). My creatinine is now up to 3.4 mg/dL, and my GFR is down to 14.4%. Oh, dear, results are not good at all. I'm being referred to a local hematologist for an injection of Aranesp. This medicine helps the hormones in the kidney drive the bone marrow to make more red blood cells. The drug must be administered by a hematologist for my insurance to cover the cost. The government also stipulates that my hemoglobin cannot be more than 10 g. I'm hoping

I'll be given an appointment soon, as I can barely function. I'm experiencing waves and waves of dizziness.

April 27, 2010

I'm given a hematologist's appointment in three weeks, but that is just not soon enough. I decide to call one of their other offices and, luckily for me, I get an appointment for today. Much, much better. I'm looking forward to some relief from the injection.

It was certainly a nice oncology/hematology office with beautiful murals on the walls, and the staff was exceptionally friendly. I looked around and saw several women without hair. Cancer patients. Hmmm. I have never been to an office like this before.

After my blood is drawn, I am seen by one of the doctors. He takes a history and does a physical examination. He tells me he can't give me the injection because my hemoglobin isn't low enough and Medicare won't pay for it. Provider's cost is $3,400 per injection. The doctor also says that since my complaints are of a rapid pulse and heart palpitations, he may want me to see a cardiologist. The doctor questions if I get night sweats and I said I do. So after seeing him, the technician draws extra blood to look for other blood cancers. Just what I need! I'm really not too happy when I leave the office. No shot and still no energy. It seems as if I'm sleeping my life away. The doctor wants to see me back in his office on May 17 to go over the findings.

I am very frustrated. And I am so upset that Medicare has control over when I can get an injection that would improve my health. I believe that when clinical symptoms like mine are present, the "hemoglobin of 10 g maximum" rule should not apply.

I decide not to wait for my May 17 return visit (at which time the doctor will probably refer me to a cardiologist) and call Dr. Diamond's office to find out which cardiology group he recommends. I'm told he suggests a certain group, and I call and make an appointment with one of their doctors for May 4.

May 4, 2010

I meet my cardiologist today and like him immediately. He, too, thinks my heart palpitations and higher pulse rate are because of my anemia. My EKG is normal. He suggests a 24-hour heart monitor if I begin to feel worse.

May 12, 2010

I return to see my hematologist to get the results of my tests. Fortunately, all but one comes back negative. My liver function test is slightly elevated. Hmm, now why is that? Again, he recommends going back to my family doctor and waiting until my hemoglobin drops to 10 g before I can return for the Aranesp injection.

May 19, 2010

Because climbing steps is getting harder and harder for me to do and the fact that my liver test is abnormal, I wonder if it's my cholesterol medication. The paperwork that comes with the medication recommends a liver function test periodically because sometimes this medicine affects the muscles. I call Dr. Diamond, and he agrees that I should stop the cholesterol medication "for now." I'm very glad I had the blood tests done.

June 6, 2010

An awful day for me! The room goes around and around…even when I'm lying in bed with my head flat. I'm sleeping every two hours and have absolutely no appetite. Maybe my hemoglobin dropped again. I need to go back to the hematologist.

June 8, 2010

At my appointment today, I learn that my hemoglobin actually dropped from 11.2 gm. to 9.8 gm. in four weeks. The hematologist said I now qualify for Aranesp. Finally. I'm given the injection and told that Medicare will pay for it. I was so grateful when I left his office. I know it isn't a good sign that I now need this medicine, but at least I'll have some energy to work my business and not drag so throughout the day.

June 21, 2010

At this hematologist's appointment, my blood is drawn again. When the doctor comes into my room, he is absolutely elated. My hemoglobin went from 9.8 g up to 12.1 g. "Unbelievable!" he says. "Every once in a while, there's a patient who responds to this medicine this quickly," and apparently, I am that rare patient. So now, I won't need the injection until my hemoglobin drops once again to 10 g or below. Resolving my anemia problem should also resolve my high pulse problem.

July 7, 2010

Another appointment with Dr. Diamond today. My creatinine is now up to 3.5 mg/dL and my GFR is down to 13.9. I'm feeling much better since my injection of Aranesp, but I still do sleep a lot. He adds another diagnosis to my original diagnosis, so I'm able to receive another injection, as my hemoglobin has already dropped. He calls the hematologist's office to arrange it.

Dr. Diamond wants me taken off the "On Hold" transplant list and placed on the "Active" transplant list. Hmm...another step closer toward transplant. It's almost three years since I was first listed, November 30, 2007. Dr. Diamond is surprised to learn that it's been that long.

Dr. Diamond now gives me guidelines for when "the call" comes through with a cadaver kidney offer. He says it often happens in the wee hours of the morning because that's when car accidents usually occur. He tells me what questions to ask to find out if it is a "good" kidney. Wow! That's a big decision for me to make. A little frightening, too. I know we're all faced with choices in life, but this one will be a life-threatening one for me. I don't know if I even know enough to make a good decision.

Should a kidney offer come through for me, the transplant coordinator has one hour to reach me by phone. If I can't be reached by that time, she must contact the next person on the list. I'm told it's okay to ask questions about the donor at this time. Usually, several hours will go by between the call and the time I'm to report to the hospital.

July 8, 2010

Madeline calls to tell me I need to have several tests done before I can become "Active," so I proceed once again to make all the necessary doctor appointments.

July 19, 2010

I have a stress test done at the cardiologist's office today. It isn't quite as bad as I remember the first one to be, but I'm glad to put it behind me.

July 27, 2010

Today, I saw my OB/GYN for an exam and Pap smear. She wished me well, said she would pray for me, and as with all the other times before, it was such a positive visit. She did take a long look at me before she left the room — as if she was seeing me for the last time. But I'll be back!

July 28, 2010

I look forward to today's visit with Madeline and the surgeons. I have so many questions to ask. Also, I'm anxious to get actively listed again. Having kidney disease has been a part of my life since I was 21 years old and just knowing I have the problem is an awful weight on my shoulders. I face the future with some trepidation, but I am also very excited knowing that a kidney transplant can make me feel so much better. As usual, Don comes along with me for support, and he also wants to ask some of his own questions.

Madeline answers all our questions thoroughly. I don't like all that I hear, but she is being honest, and I need to face it. I know I can only get through all this with God's help. **Dear God, please give me courage.**

Also today, I meet with Seth Narins, MD, PhD, the new transplant surgeon. I like him. He seems very genuine and down-to-earth. His hands are much larger than Dr. Yang's, and since I'm not a very big person, I'm hoping that won't be a problem. I guess this is a strange detail to notice, but it is a concern of mine.

Dr. Narins was the featured speaker at this month's support group meeting. He seemed very dedicated. He said he simply loves what he does — transplanting organs to give patients a second chance at life. Hmmm, which doctor should I choose? A younger physician versus an older physician. Or maybe I won't have a choice.

September 1, 2010

Another visit with Dr. Diamond. He puts me on a different cholesterol medication, Zetia, because my cholesterol is up — 188. He also takes me off one of my hypertensive medications, thinking that perhaps this is the reason for my hot flashes and night sweats. I hope the answer is that simple. Since I'm getting my monthly blood draw for transplant after this visit, he adds a few more tests for me to have done. He does say, "No dialysis." He also says the night sweats could be from uremia. Oh, dear. Maybe I'm closer to dialysis than I care to admit.

October 4, 2010

I'm not sleeping well tonight. I have such a terrible, throbbing headache. Also, I feel the need to vomit and think that perhaps if I do, I will feel better. Maybe I didn't drink enough water again this weekend.

Don and I just completed an exhausting craft show. We were at the Apple Harvest Festival in Adams County — two long 14-hour days. We came home physically spent! The fall season is our busiest time of year, as people gear up for the Christmas holidays and gift buying goes to the top of their "to-do" list. From a business perspective, this is the worst possible time for me to get really sick.

I drink and drink the water. I take two Extra-Strength Tylenols, as the headache is really awful. I get some sleep, but it is fitful. My heart is pounding quite a bit…almost like it's fluttering at some point. Is this a heart attack? My whole chest cavity feels funny. It's very hard to explain, but it certainly doesn't feel normal. I'm wondering if this is the onset for the need of dialysis. **Oh, no! Please, God, not now. Wait at least another two weeks. I have orders to get out for my business.**

October 27, 2010

I have an appointment with Dr. Diamond today. I'm feeling just awful — my heart is pounding with an increased pulse rate, and I have hot flashes and night sweats, terrible headaches, a poor appetite and low energy. He said these are all symptoms of uremia, but headaches can also be caused by high blood pressure. He increases my blood pressure medication. My parathyroid hormone (PTH) result is now 453 pg/mL (normal range 12 to 65 pg/mL), so he increases my Zemplar medication from three times a week to one pill daily.

Zemplar, a Vitamin D analog, was made for patients with kidney failure because the kidneys cannot process regular Vitamin D.

My creatinine is now up to 4.2 mg/dL, not really that high, but high enough to possibly put me over the edge facing dialysis. A creatinine blood test is the best marker for toxins excreted by the kidneys. I am a petite person, so the number to start dialysis will be lower for me than for an average or larger-built individual.

Dr. Diamond tells me I must be my own patient advocate. He advises me to call Jeri to ask her some of my paired donor questions. I do so this afternoon, and she explains it to me further. Apparently, they run the numbers in the

Transplant Bank twice a week. I believe my blood type is O positive and this may be hindering an early transplant. An O positive blood type is less common for a recipient, making the search a little more difficult.

I'm getting less nervous and more accepting of what is to come. I believe I have the best transplant team on the East Coast, and I am very thankful for that. Confidence in your medical team is truly paramount. The number one rule for patients approaching transplantation is to research the transplant center being considered. Check out their statistics. If their surgical results are less than impressive, find out why. Was it the surgeon's technique? Was decision making by the surgeon a problem? Had there been a staff turnover, whereby the personnel had not yet had time to mesh as a team? These are just a few of the possibilities, but finding the best transplant center and the best transplant team for you are extremely important for the success of your surgery.

CHAPTER 6

Telling Others

Wʜᴇɴ ʏᴏᴜ sʜᴀʀᴇ deeply personal news with friends, you probably watch their reactions a little too closely. I have deliberately kept my health issues private because I'm feeling well and looking well. I know I have some time before symptoms appear and I begin to feel and look sick. Perhaps you are apprehensive about telling your friends. Will they treat you differently? Will they even understand? How will it affect your relationship?

During my next visit to Bethlehem, I decide to talk to several of my closest friends during lunch. I'm nervous about their reactions and surprise at their responses. Perhaps it was just the shock of the news that left them so quiet. But I'll always remember what each friend said to me, who said nothing, who hugged me, and who said they would keep me in their prayers. Their remarks will remain with me forever.

July 8, 2009

This evening, I attend a class at my local library on "How to Write Your Personal Memoirs." I speak with the teacher after class. I tell her I'm on the National Kidney Transplant List and am currently keeping a diary of my journey, which I hope someday to turn into a book. I ask if she knows of someone who may want to co-author it with me. I was also hoping she would suggest a publishing company or two that I could check into. But actually, she's of little help, suggesting I should be the one to write the book, and kindly wishes me well. This made me even more determined to write my book!

I hate to tell people that I'm on the list — they look at me with so much sympathy and as if they're looking at someone who is about to die. I really don't need sympathy. Empathy, yes; sympathy, no.

July 27, 2009

I'm in Bethlehem this weekend while Don is enjoying the annual air show in Oshkosh, WI. He loves airplanes and is taking lessons towards getting his pilot's license. In packing the car to return home today, our neighbor, Jim, approaches me, and we begin talking. We discuss Don's flying interests and I mention that his friend, Wayne, transports organs to various hospitals for transplantation. He donates his plane, his gas, and his time. Now, isn't that a wonderful way to give of your time and talents? Maybe someday Wayne will deliver my new kidney to a local hospital.

Since Jim is an ICU trauma nurse at a hospital in Bethlehem, I confide in him that I am now on the National Kidney Transplant List. He listens intently and is very encouraging. I'm so glad I said something to him. Some people just know how to respond. He is very kind and says he will keep me in his prayers. He mentions that the man in the next block is a recent kidney recipient. That's nice to know. Maybe some day we can compare notes.

I realize I need to make more people aware of my kidney problem. I haven't had symptoms for the past 2½ years while on the transplant list, but I'm starting to have some now. I need to put something in the church bulletins, too, and maybe inform some of our frequent customers.

August 25, 2009

Don and I have an appointment today to meet Madeline. That's fine with me, as I haven't actually seen the transplant team in almost two years. Madeline is very nice, and I really like her. I tell her I would like to put a note in my churches' bulletins, so that others may know of my need for a kidney. She agrees that this should be done and writes out a sample paragraph for me. This certainly is a big help, as for once, I am struggling for words.

I e-mail the paragraph to Very Rev. S. David Mahaffey, Jr., the priest at St. Nicholas Russian Orthodox Church in Bethlehem. It read: "Over 100,000 people are waiting nationwide for kidney transplants. One of them is in our congregation, Carole Fair. Carole has battled kidney disease for many years, and her kidney function is now declining. She is hopeful she will be able to receive a kidney transplant before needing to start dialysis. If you would like more information, please contact Jeri Goldman, RN, CCTC, Living Donor Coordinator at Harrisburg Hospital."

*I guess there's no turning back now. People will know, and that's okay. Initially, I didn't want to tell anyone for fear they would look at me and see me only as a sick person. I need to swallow my pride and get the word out. This is the only way I'll know if there is someone out there who wants to donate a kidney to me. A very remote chance, I know, but a chance nevertheless. **Please, God, help me with this. I so need you.***

August 26, 2009

I call Rev. Fr. Timothy Hojnicki at Holy Apostles Ortho-dox Mission in Mechanicsburg and schedule a time to meet with him. When I arrive at his office, I give him the paper with the paragraph written on it and ask him to please put it in an upcoming Sunday bulletin. "Whoa!" he exclaims when he first reads it. He seems really shocked. He wishes me well and assures me he will publish it. He stresses that as a church family we need to share in each other's lives, both through the happy and the more difficult times. He says that "the church supports donation as a way to a better life" and that "hopefully, transplantation will lead to improvements in the treatment of kidney disease." It's good to learn the thoughts of the church, and it was a very favorable visit overall.

You can check into the religious views of your church by calling the Gift of Life Donor program. Refer to the *Resources* section of this book for more information.

August 28, 2009

I got a telephone call from Helen T., a member of my church in Bethlehem. She heard through the grapevine that I had kidney disease. She is a severe diabetic and also has had a kidney transplant. Helen has been in and out of the hospital many times in the past decade. She has been so sick recently that every day is a struggle for her. We talk for about a half hour and I so appreciate her phone call. It's nice to get another kidney patient's perspective on what I'm going through. I'm worried about her though and decide to keep her in my daily prayers.

Sadly, Helen passed away in May 2011.

August 30, 2009

We fly to Kansas City today for the weekend to celebrate the 90th birthday of my very favorite uncle, Uncle John (my mother's brother). I know back in Pennsylvania my short paragraph is being read in both Sunday church bulletins and the word is out. Perhaps someone will read it and may even be willing to donate their kidney to me. I'm glad that it's now out in the open. A kind word every now and then will be so appreciated by me. It's always nice to know someone cares.

February 1, 2010

I now want to tell a young friend of mine, Jeanette (Jay) Diaz, about my kidney problem. About ten years ago, as a volunteer for the Central Pennsylvania Literacy Council, I was Jay's mother's teacher. During the two years that I worked with her mother, Don and I became very impressed with Jay, so much so that we offered to sponsor her into the Milton Hershey School in Hershey. To sponsor a young woman into the school simply means that we'll mentor and befriend her. It doesn't mean, as some people think, that we'll finance her way. Once accepted into the school, Jay would be on a full scholarship. This includes tuition, room and board, medical and dental, clothing and incidentals. Absolutely everything is paid for. What a fabulous opportunity!

Jay submitted her application and then the testing began — academically, psychologically, and emotionally. The competition was very keen, but she was accepted! Jay started at the Milton Hershey School in the eighth grade and graduated from high school there with an associate's degree in graphic design/printing. She went on to the Art Institute of Pittsburgh and graduated with a major in marketing and a minor in graphic design. In 2011, she got her diploma in web design. We are so very proud of her. She had worked extremely hard, applied herself, and achieved beyond our expectations.

Since graduating from the Milton Hershey School, Jay has always called me "Mommy Carole" and Don "Daddy Don," and we have become a support family for her. I found it hard to tell her and her fiancé, Joe, about my health problems because I didn't want to worry them. But now I thought I needed to say something as I was becoming symptomatic. Jay lives in Pittsburgh, is employed, and doing well.

I wrote this e-mail to her on February 14, 2010:

"Hi there,

"I've been wanting to tell you both something, but every time you're here visiting and we get to talking, I don't say anything. It's just not an easy subject to approach.

"Jay and Joe, I am on the National Kidney Transplant List. I was placed on it on November 30, 2007. It usually takes about five years to get a kidney from the list, if you don't have a family member who is able to donate. Don can't donate because he has hypertension. I had a birth defect that slowly caused the deterioration of my kidneys, but I'm not on dialysis yet.

"I just wanted you to know. Please don't worry. I know God will take care of me and I will be okay.
Love and Hugs,
Mommy Carole"

I heard from Jay that very day:

"You should have told me! I believe we have two. I will give you one of mine. I'm healthy. What do I need to do so I can help you?"

Wow! I never expected her to say that! I was in total shock. What a dear, sweet girl — and so generous. But whoa! She needed to really think this through. It's a big decision and should not be made lightly. She needed to talk with her fiancé, her parents, her doctors, etc. And I certainly don't want her to do anything that would jeopardize her young life...for me. I best not get too excited too soon.

February 15, 2010

I call Jeri, who is now in charge of living donors, and talk with her about Jay. Jeri's so excited that I found a donor! I tell her the story of how Jay and I know each other, and Jeri said she got goose bumps. I also tell her of my concern that Jay is in her childbearing years and I'm worried that if she becomes pregnant, she will only have one kidney. Jeri tells me not to discourage her. She said she knows of young women with only one kidney who have successfully given birth. The transplant center makes it possible for Jay to meet with a high-risk obstetrician and he tells her exactly how to take care of herself should she become pregnant.

Jeri tells me that Jay needs to make the first contact, however; she could not. I e-mail Jay and give her Jeri's phone number, and Jay calls her right away. Wow! She sure didn't waste any time.

Jay e-mails me that she will be getting a call with an appointment for blood tests. The first step is to see if we're compatible. Although she lives in Pittsburgh, she will be in the area next week for her job and available for tests locally.

CHAPTER 7

Jay Gets Tested

Even when you think you've found someone who wants to donate their kidney to you, there are a number of prerequisites that must be followed. A living donor needs to be between the ages of 18 and 65. They cannot have high blood pressure, diabetes, or cancer, and they have to have a body mass index of 35 or less. Living donors do not need to be biologically related to the recipients to be considered. But like recipients, living donors need to have several diagnostic tests performed to ensure a safe outcome. Donor testing takes about 8 to 10 weeks to complete and is paid for by the recipient's insurance. The transplant office cannot share any information between donor and recipient to ensure the privacy of both.

I'm told that donor surgery is a laparoscopic procedure that takes 2 to 3 hours. The procedure involves three small incisions, each about ½", and has little discomfort and a fast recovery time. Patients are usually hospitalized for 2 to 3 days.

February 16, 2010

Jay calls and informs me that she has an appointment for February 26 at 7 a.m. at Harrisburg Hospital. We're on our way!

How do I feel? Well, I am just shocked. **Thank you, dear God. You are so good to me.** *I feel the start of such an inner peace. However, I'm realistic enough to know that this is just the beginning. I don't know Jay's blood type and I would want to make sure I'm doing the right thing for her. Joe said the decision was totally up to Jay. I told Jay that having one kidney may become a problem during pregnancy. She said she wasn't worried about that, as they only wanted one child.*

The very fact that she wants to do this for me moves me to tears. I just can't believe it. If she ever wanted to thank me for what I did for her in her young life, she found no better way than to give me more of my own life to look forward to. Even if Jay and I aren't a match, she has given me hope, and I am just overwhelmed by her kindness. She said, "It's no big deal," but to me, it absolutely is! Again and again, **thank you, dear God.** *Tonight, I wear my cross necklace when I go to sleep. I always do this when I want to feel closer to God and when I'm especially grateful for something. And I'm so grateful for this young woman.*

February 26, 2010

I meet Jay at Harrisburg Hospital. Rather, we bump into each other as we walk between the two areas of the complex, Harrisburg Hospital and Brady Hall, going in opposite directions. It is a cold, snowy day, with traffic and roads a major problem. It is 8:30 a.m., and Jay was scheduled to have her blood drawn at 7 a.m. She is late because of the roads and a highway accident, but I'm just so glad to see her. Apparently, it doesn't matter to the technicians at the hospital lab, as they just draw her blood when she gets there.

Jay has blood drawn for blood typing and a fasting blood sugar. To test for diabetes, she is given sugar water to drink. We sit in the waiting room and wait for two hours to pass, at which time another blood sample is drawn. Her grandparents have diabetes and her mother is a borderline diabetic, so we are hoping to rule out diabetes for Jay. Time goes by quickly. Jay and I talk nonstop and learn a lot more about each other. She's a pretty neat young woman, strong and opinionated, but maturing nicely.

After the blood work is drawn, we head back to Transplant Services to meet with Jeri. She takes Jay's blood pressure and asks her a few questions and then sits down to talk to both of us. Well, unfortunately, the news is not good. We are not a match. In fact, we couldn't be further from matching. I learn that I'm an O Positive and can only receive a kidney from an O donor. Jay is an AB Positive and can give to anyone other than an O recipient. So very disappointing! So what does all this mean? Will my chance for a new kidney just become wishful thinking? I really don't know.

Jeri explains. She said if Jay chooses to go ahead with this, she would recommend we get placed on the Paired Donor List. I was currently on the National Kidney Trans-

plant List only and for a cadaver kidney. Since it seemed as if Jay wanted to proceed, the next step (if her blood sugars were okay) would be for her to return for a half-day of extensive testing. Should she become "approved" after testing, the Paired Donor List would be the way for us to go. It would allow a kidney to be found for me and a recipient to be found for Jay's kidney as well, all from a very large data bank.

Jeri's talk with us was quite educational. I learned that the number of available organs has actually diminished over the past 15 years. We now have air bags in our automobiles and people are wearing seat belts, so the number of deaths as a result of car accidents has actually decreased. Also, years ago, people didn't know they had high blood pressure until they arrived at the hospital with a stroke or heart attack. Upon death, their hearts, lungs, and kidneys would be donated. We all know now about the dangers of hypertension, so strokes are far less likely to occur. That's certainly great news for the individual, but it's not good news for patients awaiting transplants.

Jay and I return to my home…very disappointed, of course, but well, we tried. I make lunch for us, and we sit down to eat and Don joins us. We tell him all that has happened at the hospital, and most importantly, I tell him we are not a match.

I told a number of my friends that I had someone who wanted to donate their kidney to me. They were very excited for me. I must now tell them that Jay and I are not a match. I will keep praying though and, hopefully, something positive may still happen.

March 1, 2010

Some days I wonder if a transplant will ever come about for me. What if Jay becomes pregnant at a time when my need for a transplant is the greatest? If we are on the Paired Donor List, she would have to be removed from the list for the nine months of her pregnancy plus time for infant care, and I would have to be taken off as well. Perhaps with a young child, she would no longer want to donate. This, and other scenarios, run through my mind. It's depressing for me. I make myself stop thinking and simply appeal to God for His help. The road to a kidney transplant is such an emotional roller coaster.

March 4, 2010

Jay calls and tells me she is not diabetic and now plans to continue with the tests to donate her kidney to someone else. I still can't believe she is going through with this. The next time she will be in this area for her job will be April 29, so Jeri makes an appointment that day for her to undergo more tests. Once she has been cleared, we will be placed on the Paired Donor List. I tell her I will meet her again at the hospital. I need to support her in every way I can; it's the very least I can do.

April 29, 2010

Jay has her full day of tests today at Harrisburg Hospital beginning at 7:30 a.m.

She meets first with Jeri, then Dr. Yang, the social worker, and the financial counselor. I arrive at Transplant Services at about 8:30 a.m., but she is already in the office, so I sit in the waiting room. I'm just not able to move too quickly in the mornings. It used to be my favorite time of day, a time when I accomplished the most, but not so now.

Jay and I head to the lab for a barrage of blood tests. She then meets with a high-risk obstetrician for a consultation. He talks to her about the precautions that must be taken should she become pregnant, the problems with infections, etc. It's an interesting and thorough talk. I keep waiting for Jay to get cold feet, but she doesn't seem to be backing out of this at all. God bless her!

I mention to Jay that she is really saving my life, and she just says, "What goes around, comes around, Mom."

I was very moved by her kindness, and then I recalled how she had adopted her stepbrother when she was only 20 years old and just out of college. She saw the need to support him because of his home situation, and she did. She was so determined to help him. No one could change her mind on that, either.

The last scheduled test for Jay is a CT scan of the abdomen and pelvis. Dye is injected into her vein to get a better contrast. When she leaves Nuclear Medicine, her face is all red and she's blowing her nose. I comment, "Were you crying, honey?" And she says, "No!" We leave Nuclear Medicine and walk to the restroom. When she comes out, her eyes are both red and swollen, so we rush back to Nuclear Medicine. The nurse tells us that Jay had a reaction to the dye and should wait in the room for one hour; this, at 12:30 p.m. when Jay hasn't had anything to eat since 7:30 a.m. The nurse gives Jay a snack to hold her over and then gives her medication for the allergy. She warns Jay that in the future she is to tell medical personnel she's allergic to the dye, as each episode could get worse and become quite serious.

We leave the hospital at about 1:30 p.m. and head to Denny's, her choice, for a much-needed lunch. I'm so relieved to put all this behind me. We come back to my home, where she promptly lies down and falls asleep. The stress of the day and the allergy medication has taken its toll. She sleeps well and departs for her home at about 5 p.m. What a day we've had! I feel so sorry for her. She sure went through a lot — a lot of poking, x-rays, and consults. I hope it is not for naught. We'll have the results of today's tests in about 5 to 7 days.

May 6, 2010

Most of Jay's test results are in and they're looking really good. The GFR test was done to determine the "strength" of her kidneys, and she said the result was in the 130s (average is 85). It must be great to be young! Now she'll go back to her doctor in Pittsburgh for a Pap test and forward that result to Transplant Services.

May 12, 2010

It's my understanding that once all the test results are in, our paperwork then goes to the Selection Committee. The evaluation goal of this committee is always for the safety and well-being of the potential donor. They never let their judgment be clouded by the desire to improve the welfare of the recipient. Any detected risk to the current or future health of the donor must be ruled out — even if the potential donor is willing to proceed.

All kidney patients are discussed by the Selection Committee, even those who were transplanted previously and are in need of another kidney. This is the same detailed process adhered to for the National Kidney

Transplant List. The committee discusses Jay and me as individuals, and if accepted, we would be placed on the Paired Donor List. Our entry on the list would become formal when I'd receive a letter informing me that we were both accepted. It's a good thing my GFR was at 14.4% and not any lower, as this all takes some time.

I sign the form, "Transplant Recipient Consent for National Paired Exchange Program." Jeri tells me that one blood test remains outstanding for Jay. I e-mail her as a reminder and she says she will have the blood drawn soon.

September 6, 2010
This week Jay is working locally again. She is scheduled to have her blood drawn for that particular test on September 10 at Harrisburg Hospital. Good news.

September 13, 2010
I e-mail Jay to find out if she had her blood drawn. She told me her great-grandmother is very ill, so she didn't have time to go to Harrisburg Hospital. I hope it isn't because she doesn't want to donate her kidney. I live with that fear every day, ever since Jeri told me that possible donors can, and sometimes do, back out at the last minute. After they have gone through all the tests and are asked to sign the paper giving permission to take their kidney for transplant, they can't do it, and everything gets canceled. What a disappointment that must be for the recipient!

September 14, 2010
Jay will be working locally again next week, and she'll have time to visit us. I look forward to seeing her. She has also been in contact with Jeri, who rescheduled her to have

her blood drawn at that time. I sure hope this happens. I really want to be on the Paired Donor List, but until this last test is done, I know I'm not.

September 22, 2010
  Jay stops by for a visit. She just came from Harrisburg Hospital, where she had her blood drawn for that final test. So glad that was done! I hope to hear from Jeri soon, and I hope to hear from her with good news.

October 1, 2010
  Yes! Jay and I have been accepted by the Selection Committee. Jeri calls Jay to tell her she has been approved as a donor, meaning also that the committee considers it safe for her to donate. Jay had signed her paperwork previously, so we're finally on the Paired Donor List. What an achievement! So now I'm on two lists, one for a cadaver kidney and one for a live kidney. My chances for a new kidney have just doubled. Hopefully, one of these lists will come through for me.

I have a feeling it's in the nick of time. I just have a feeling…

CHAPTER 8

Financial and Psychosocial Assessments

Many evaluations are done to help kidney recipients and their families prepare for a transplant. Obviously, this transition has been well thought out, assessing all angles, and I'm so glad that that's the case. It makes the journey to transplant an easier path to follow.

November 5, 2008

Don and I attend this month's support group meeting, where both insurance and social counselors are present. They give a fair presentation, but I still have many questions. What is the best insurance plan for someone like me on the transplant list? How much out-of-pocket money will Don and I have to pay? I'm sure you would want to know these answers, too. Sometimes the more I know, the more I realize I need to know, so when one question is answered, three more pop up.

I am now looking at Medicare insurance, as I will turn 65 years of age on May 8, 2009. It is so complicated. I have to make sure I have enough drug coverage to pay for my prescriptions during and after transplant. Then there's the donut hole. After researching four different companies and becoming totally confused, I make my decision…and I hope I've chosen the right plan. Only time will tell.

August 25, 2009

I have another appointment today at Transplant Services. After meeting with Madeline, we meet with our financial coordinator. This visit is so worthwhile for us. She talks to us about PACENET, the governmental prescription coverage for older citizens, and other governmental plans which may help defray the costs of my medicines. My medications are definitely on the increase, both in number and in cost. We need to fill out a PACENET application and, hopefully, we'll get approved.

I speak with the Transplant Services social worker today as well. The issues we discuss help assess my survival and have a bearing on my ability to cope with the entire transplant process. The assessment is not conducted to determine my social worth or to list me according to some rank. Questions are asked to assess social support within my family, as well as if I have any psychopathology, compliance history, or substance abuse problems. It's a very thorough assessment.

Our social worker feels we are doing everything right, "just try and stay the course."

September 4, 2009
Today we learn we have been accepted by PACENET.
How very nice! This will be a big help for us this year, as
it will pay for a portion of our premiums and a portion of
our co-pays. This acceptance, however, is for one year only.
Next year, we'll have to apply again.

In January 2011, we applied to PACENET and submitted our taxes for 2010. During that year, Don and I needed to put a new roof on our house. We withdrew money out of savings and that raised our income level. Sadly, the year we needed PACENET the most, 2011, we were denied.

It is difficult for me to explain the many health plans available out there and which one may be best for you. As I write this book, governmental changes are occurring often and these changes can definitely affect the payments of many plans. The financial aspect of your transplant surgery can be discussed in more detail with the financial coordinator at your transplant center. Just know that this is made available to each patient facing transplantation.

CHAPTER 9

Dialysis or Transplant?

WE ALL WANT the best life possible for ourselves. I have such a respect for life, have never taken it for granted, and have always played hard and worked hard. I certainly want my life to count for something as well. But sometimes I wonder...how am I to decide if I should even go for a kidney transplant (with all its risks), or stay on home dialysis (with all its inconveniences) for the rest of my life? I really didn't know anything about dialysis.

During one visit with Dr. Diamond, I told him this, and he immediately picked up the phone and spoke with a nurse at the dialysis center. He made an appointment for us to get together to talk. I could ask her all my questions at that time. I was so relieved. Knowledge is a wonderful thing — it helps you make a more informed decision.

June 12, 2009

I have an appointment today with Maryellen Och, RN, CNN, the dialysis nurse at Fresenius Medical Care. This dialysis facility had just opened in our area in February 2009, and Dr. Diamond is its medical director. Maryellen and I spend almost two hours talking together, at which time she explains many things to me and clears up some concerns I have. Truly enlightening! She offers to show me the room where hemodialysis takes place, but I don't want to see it. I just can't look, simply too frightening for me.

Dialysis is a filtering procedure used to treat kidney failure. It actually does some of the things a normal kidney does, such as removing extra water from the body and removing waste products that build up in the bloodstream. There are two kinds of dialysis — hemodialysis and peritoneal dialysis. Hemodialysis is most often done in a clinic by trained health professionals who can watch for any problems and it involves needles. It's done for a shorter amount of time and on fewer days each week than peritoneal dialysis.

Peritoneal dialysis gives you more freedom than hemodialysis. It can be done at home or in any clean place, and you can do it when you travel. It doesn't require as many food and fluid restrictions as hemodialysis and it does not use needles. However, there are risks to both. Let your doctor help you decide which one is best for you. No matter which form of therapy Dr. Diamond chooses for me, I know I will have a team of health care professionals available to meet my needs — a doctor, a nurse, a dietitian, and a social worker.

In Europe, the United Kingdom and Canada, most kidney patients elect to do continuous cycling peritoneal dialysis (CCPD) at home. This is a slower, more natural process for the body. Very few patients in these areas are even offered hemodialysis. In the United States, however, kidney patients tend to choose hemodialysis because of greater convenience and less personal responsibility. CCPD is the method of choice by physicians, as it gives the patient daily dialysis versus the three times weekly dialysis at the clinics.

Maryellen is very personable. She seems quite caring, which is important to me, especially as my kidney function continues to deteriorate. Her sense of humor is so uplifting, and I would have no qualms calling her with any further questions or concerns. She gives me two books to read and her business card. I will carry her business card in my wallet at all times. Perhaps when I see her again, it will be when there's a real need. Maybe when my creatinine reaches 4 mg/dL or so, dialysis will be in the picture. (Of course, I really have no idea what the number will actually be.)

I ask Maryellen about the life span of transplanted kidneys. She tells me that kidneys from living donors usually last about 20 years, and kidneys from deceased donors usually last about 10 to 15 years. A transplanted kidney can reject tomorrow, next month, or several years from now. And sometimes without any symptoms. Now that's scary!

The benefits of a living kidney donation, in addition to longevity, are that the wait time would be significantly shorter than on the deceased donor list, and surgery would be scheduled (so I could plan for family, work, pets, etc.) The benefits for a live donor are twofold: a complete medi-

cal examination which may find some unknown medical issue not otherwise detected and the emotional benefit of helping someone else.

Maryellen stresses to me that transplantation is a treatment, not a cure for kidney disease. I found that interesting, as I had always thought otherwise. I learn, too, that not everyone is automatically a candidate for transplant.

It will take a lifelong commitment on my part to care for my transplanted kidney with daily medications, frequent blood draws, and frequent clinic appointments. The benefits of transplantation include better health, improved quality and length of life, no need for dialysis, and enjoyment of a higher level of energy. However, there are risks to transplant surgery. These include anesthesia risk, infection, rejection (acute or chronic), blood clots in my legs, cardiac complications, the need to take medications as long as the transplant functions, depression or anxiety, and a higher risk of some cancers. The alternative to transplant is, of course, dialysis, proper diet, and medications.

June 27, 2009

Now that I'm 65 years old, I begin to look at my life from a slightly different perspective. I wonder how many years I may have left. Will I be taking a kidney from someone who may have a longer life span than I? I don't know; no one knows. Yet just being human, I want to live as long as God will allow. Because of my stature, 5'2" and 122 pounds, perhaps I'll get a kidney from a child, which is even more difficult to think about. The decision isn't mine to make, I tell myself, it is God's. And I need to just leave it in His hands.

I am sometimes asked by my friends, "Who is your doctor?" I tell them that I have quite a few, but I add that it takes a team of professionals with many dedicated individuals to bring about a positive end result in this journey. Each one's role is so important, and they all have to work well together as a team. I realize the true value of the team I'm with and am ever so thankful for each of them.

One of the primary goals of a transplant team is to educate the patient because knowing what is happening and what to expect is more than half the battle. That's why the statistics for success at PinnacleHealth Transplant Services are so high. The transplant team cares about the patient and gives excellent support and training all along the way. Most transplant centers have personnel that are this conscientious.

CHAPTER 10

Dialysis!

Those of you who are on dialysis probably remember just how you felt in the days leading up to this treatment. I'll never forget my time just prior to dialysis. It remains forever in my memory bank.

October 12, 2010

For the past week, I have been really sick. I have had absolutely no appetite — I can go the entire day without a bite of food. I force myself to eat because if I don't, I know I will rapidly lose weight, weight that I can't afford to lose. My nights are the worst. The night sweats are so bad. My neck and upper chest, even my arms, are coated with sweat. I finally give in and call Dr. Diamond today and leave a message with his receptionist. I have put it off as long as I possibly can because I know what he will say. He will recommend dialysis.

I'm coming out of the bank when my cell phone rings. I'll never forget that call. "Dr. Diamond says he can't do anything more for you," the receptionist tells me. "He's recommending dialysis." It should have come as no surprise to me, but it does. All my life I've feared dialysis and that's exactly what I'm facing now. What else can be done? Nothing else. Dialysis is the only way to get rid of the toxins in my body. Just the type of dialysis may remain my choice.

I ask her what the next step is and she says she'll get back to me. I turn my cell phone off and begin to cry. So it has finally come to this — dialysis! I'm angry that my body has let me down. I need a bit more time to switch from feelings of such despair to being thankful that I can be alive through whatever means are now available. This was not always the case with kidney failure.

One question remained for me: "Why wasn't I retaining fluid?" My ankles weren't swollen. I always thought I would fill up with fluid before dialysis would become necessary. Hmm…interesting. I guess my body is just not reacting that way.

The receptionist calls me back to tell me Dr. Diamond wants me to have a consultation with a surgeon. He recommends a general surgeon in Harrisburg and I okay the appointment.

Surgery has to be scheduled to create an opening inside my abdominal cavity for placement of a peritoneal dialysis (PD) catheter, a soft plastic tube. The catheter would have a titanium tip on the outside end for attachment to the PD machine. When not in use, this 9" catheter would be taped to the outside of my belly. The catheter would be used to fill and drain the peritoneal cavity of solution. Sounded awful! But with time, I knew I would learn to accept this.

It's such a down time for me and no one really to talk to. I feel so all alone. I know Don, my nearest and dearest, is always there for me, but I need to talk with another kidney patient, someone who really understands what I'm going through because they've been there, too.

When you're tempted to give up, it's always a good idea to confide in someone. Reach out to a family member or a friend. A shared problem is a solved problem.

October 19, 2010

Up until now, I have always been positive. That's simply my nature. I am rarely down. But now, I'm depressed. I know I should snap out of it and could, if I really made myself. But for now, I choose not to smile or to look on the "bright side of things." I am well aware that I have the ability to reframe my negative thoughts into positive ones. I know a positive outlook helps me defend against stress, which negatively impacts my immune system and emotional and physical health. All that good stuff! But I also know my survival instincts will kick in when it's time, and I will be in there fighting, fighting hard. I am a strong woman. But until then, I just want to feel sorry for myself.

My illness has been such a long road — so many daily medicines; a difficult low-protein, low-salt diet; always mindful to drink nine glasses of water each day; watching for worsening symptoms; doctor and lab appointments galore; and always, decisions and more decisions to make. Just a lot of stress in general. It sort of weighs a person down after awhile. Maintaining a positive and independent attitude isn't always easy. Nor does it make a transplant happen any sooner. Here I am, about to go on home dialysis, even after being on the National Kidney Transplant List for almost three years and recently, the Paired Donor List. I fear that a big problem was not being activated until just two months ago, when my health began to really deteriorate. Perhaps I should have been taken off "On Hold" much earlier, like months before.

I continue to carry my cell phone faithfully whenever I go outside my home, as I was told to do by Madeline. When it rings, I always think, "Is this a call telling me they've found a kidney for me?" "Is this really it?" And always, always, I am disappointed.

November 1, 2010

I receive a call from Maryellen today. We have a long conversation and she is so encouraging. I need and appreciate encouragement so much right now.

My PD catheter surgery is scheduled for this week and I am ready. I just hope I can hang in there until the PD catheter wound heals and I can begin dialysis. Dr. Diamond wants me to learn CCPD for home use. Maryellen schedules our week-long training session at the dialysis center beginning Monday, November 29. Each day, I'll spend about four hours with her, learning the manual method as well as the cycler method. I'm ready for this, too. I'm tired of feeling sick all the time. The session will end with Maryellen visiting our home to check on the specific area where my machine and supplies will be.

For those of you who don't know how peritoneal dialysis works, let me explain. The peritoneum is the space within your abdomen. A thin lining called the peritoneal membrane covers this space inside your body, and this membrane acts as a dialyzer for your blood. With dialysis, a special fluid called dialysate is put into the peritoneum and stays there for several hours. Then the waste products and extra water move through the peritoneal membrane into the dialysate. The dialysate is drained away and replaced with fresh dialysate. I will be hooked up to the cycler (the home dialysis machine) through my abdomen for this process every night. I will begin with nine hours of dialysis each night.

A year ago, I couldn't even say the word "dialysis" without cringing. I know acceptance is the first step to overcoming, and I have accepted the fact that I won't be lucky enough to get someone's kidney before I need dialysis. But I pray to God that with time, I will some day get a new kidney.

It takes courage to be a patient, it really does. And I firmly believe this. I often wonder how patients without a medical background can even understand all this. It must be most difficult for them. To put a lay person in a medical situation where they have a fair amount of responsibility for their own health, as with kidney failure, must be simply overwhelming for some. My medical background allows me to look at my kidney problem differently than people without medical knowledge. In some ways, this may work to my advantage, and perhaps in other ways, it may not.

November 4, 2010

Today is my catheter placement surgery. I never thought I'd look forward to it as I am. I just want to move forward. I'm really feeling lousy, but with this catheter placement,

I'm hopeful that eventually dialysis will improve my health.
Lord, I need you. Please keep me strong.

We report to Harrisburg Hospital today for the 9 a.m. surgery. Don, of course, is with me. Whatever would I do without him? He is such a faithful and loving husband. Following the surgery, I awake in the RR with a large dressing over my entire belly. I'm told not to take a full bath or shower, just a bird bath, for 11 days. I will see the surgeon at that time and the dressing will be removed. It's going to be a long 11 days.

Life will probably never be the same for me. My attitude is good at this point; I don't want to be sick any more and I'm ready to accept dialysis. There's really no choice. A constant prayer of mine is that I will make it to home dialysis and not get so sick that I will need hemodialysis before the home dialysis can be started. The surgeon tells me my numbers are going up quickly. I guess he means my creatinine. Not good. **Please, Lord, help me to hang in there for another three weeks! Hemodialysis would be the very worst thing that could happen to me now.**

November 7, 2010

I'm awakened by a severe headache, nausea, and vomiting. "Get me to the ER, Don." It's 5:15 a.m., and I feel like my head is going to explode. He takes me to Harrisburg Hospital's ER, where the questions begin, an IV is put in, and blood is drawn. They do a CT scan of the brain and fortunately for me, that's negative. The nephrologist on call is not Dr. Diamond, but a woman doctor whose name I cannot pronounce. I ask that she please call Dr. Diamond, as I have been his patient for seven years, whereas she doesn't even know me. I doubt that she will. My blood pressure is high, *so they give me an extra dose of antihypertensive medication and antinausea medication, and discharge me. I have the choice of staying overnight to determine further the cause of my headache, but I choose to leave. Once I arrive home, the headache subsides. I have always been susceptible to headaches, dating back to migraines during my menopause years. I have learned to work through them the best I can.*

It was a long week — some days were good, some were not. I thought this was just the way it was going to be until I went on dialysis. Dr. Diamond wanted me started as soon as possible, according to Maryellen, and he prescribed a regimen of kidney dialysis. She called me from the dialysis center to see how I was doing after the surgery. She offered to remove my dressing (oh, thank you!) in a few days and an appointment was made. I was afraid to see what was under the dressing. It's going to be an awful sight, but just another thing I have to get used to. And then, at the very least, I'll be able to shower.

I don't understand all the problems with other organ failures, but it sure seems to me that the kidney does a lot of different things within our bodies, more than I had ever imagined. So when this organ begins to fail, a patient experiences a lot of symptoms. And each kidney patient experiences them differently. I may react one way with symptoms, yet someone else's reaction may be completely different. We each travel our own personal journey and have our own special story to tell.

November 15, 2010

I see the surgeon today. He removes my stitches and says my incisions look good. I look down at my belly and see this catheter protruding out and want to cry. I bite my lip. We talk a little about how to care for my belly. He releases me, and tells me I can now only take showers, no baths while on dialysis. I long for the day when I can once again enjoy the luxury of a bath and relaxing in the tub. But will that day ever come for me?

November 17, 2010

Don and I experience the first-time home delivery of my medical supplies. We are shocked beyond words. Our mouths literally drop open! A huge truck pulls up to our house, and a young man lowers the truck's back gate and begins loading box after box after box onto the dolly. There are 92 items in total, many for the first and only time, like a blood pressure cuff, a thermometer, etc. The boxes that contain the bags of dialysis fluid are only a two-week supply.

And this delivery didn't even include the actual cycler machine and machine table. These were delivered the next day via FedEx.

The boxes are very heavy. Don's concerned that their weight may effect the floorboards of our house, so he carefully has the driver distribute the boxes evenly throughout the room. I'm so glad he's home. I would have had no idea where to put it all, other than in our bedroom. I decide to call Maryellen because I'm thinking there surely must be some mistake. We got so many supplies! She assures me no mistake was made. Now I'll truly be living off a machine.

November 18, 2010

Today (Friday), the pain in my belly is very bad. The PD catheter is poking me terribly. It makes sitting and *walking very difficult. I call the surgeon and tell him my problem. He says that when I'm dialyzed for the first time on Monday, he hopes the fluid comes out readily and that it isn't blocked by the position of the PD catheter. If there is a blockage, I'm to call him.*

November 22, 2010

Maryellen and I embark on our first day of dialysis training. She teaches me the manual method. Should the electricity go off in our home or should we be traveling and unable to take the cycler with us, this is how I'm to do dialysis. Each treatment is considered an exchange. The fluid comes out quickly. I don't seem to have a problem, so there's no need to call the surgeon.

*I'm overwhelmed by the procedure. **Lord, I have no idea how I'll ever be able to do this! Please don't leave me.** So many steps are involved, and they must be done using an almost-sterile technique to prevent peritonitis (an infection in the abdominal cavity). It all seems so very difficult to me.*

Maryellen is very patient and extremely knowledgeable. Not only is she that, but she's also able to get information across to me well as any teacher. She has been a dialysis nurse for 22 years. I'm very lucky to have her as my dialysis nurse.

November 23, 2010

Don came home from bear hunting last evening and comes with me to class today. What a difference he makes! I feel more secure, and I don't have to concentrate so hard on every word Maryellen says. I practice today what I learned yesterday.

Maryellen introduces the cycler to me and demonstrates how it works. I think I can learn this. It's a little easier than the manual method. So many tubes are involved, though. When I set this up in my bedroom at home, I will need a line that extends from me into our bathroom and empties into the toilet. This is the way I would rid myself of the toxins.

I'm still having problems with my PD catheter. It simply hurts and, again, walking remains difficult. Maryellen doesn't drain the fluid in me completely between exchanges to allow the catheter to float and to be less painful. She believes additional surgery is not necessarily the answer, as it doesn't always correct the problem and it subjects me to possible infection. She thinks we can work around the problem, and I sure hope so.

November 24, 2010

Don comes with me again today. What a great support person! Bless him. I try to set up the cycler, but need so many prompts from Maryellen, it's discouraging. I still don't know how I'll ever be able to master this, but I guess doing something every day for the rest of my life will make me an expert eventually. I'm having trouble catching on. I believe it's because I'm being taught by listening and I'm a visual learner. I need to see the instructions and pictures. Maryellen is going to get me some picture cards, and that should be a big help for me.

Connecting to the cycler is easier for me to write about than it certainly was for me to do initially. Before each exchange, any changes needing to be made to my regimen would be done in the "My Settings" mode of the cycler. (Ah! the joy of computers.) I then gather all my supplies and mask and wash my hands thoroughly. A tubing/film cassette is pressed into place in the machine and the door is securely closed. When directed by the cycler, I start connecting my bags, ensuring that the heater bag is placed evenly on the heater tray/scale. When prompted by the machine, I break the cones on the heater and solution bags with my fingers, bending back and forth until completely separated and the fluid flows freely. I clamp unused lines, verify that all bag connections match those on the screen, and let the cycler flush the solution/drain the lines. After making sure the patient line clamp is open, I prime it and then close it. Ensuring both my catheter and patient line clamps are closed, I use aseptic technique to connect my PD catheter to the machine. Once connected, both catheter and patient line clamps are opened, and my treatment begins. I can now remove my mask. The number of times I cycle through Drain, Fill, and Dwell (or Pause) depends on my prescribed therapy. The cycler will automatically take me through my prescription. Different people drain differently, so adjustments may need to be made from time to time.

November 26, 2010

I had yesterday off (Thanksgiving) and needed it. Now I'm back in class, but without any energy and simply dragging. Don left this morning to go deer hunting, and I concentrate once again on the task before me. I hook myself to the cycler and everything is going well until I need to use the bathroom. We have to disconnect everything and start all over again. Unlike some patients, I'm still able to urinate. Maryellen is going to make sure I have a connector extension to prevent such a problem from occurring again. More tubes!

November 29, 2010

Maryellen and I continue working with the cycler. The key for success with this class is practice, practice, and more practice. I make patience my friend.

November 30, 2010

And again today, I hook up to the cycler. For whatever reason, the steps to this procedure are just not connecting yet for me. Machines and I don't see eye to eye. If Don were here, he'd learn very quickly. He's so good at understanding and handling machines.

It's difficult teaching someone with kidney disease, as the patient suffers from short-term memory loss, a very real side effect and a well-known problem of ESRD. It makes learning all the more difficult for the patient. Maryellen realizes this, of course, but that doesn't make it any easier for me. I have a poor memory now, thanks to kidney disease.

Hmm, November 30 — now that's a familiar date. Ah, yes, it was three years ago today that I was first put on the National Kidney Transplant List. And so far, I haven't gotten even one phone call with a kidney offer. They say it won't happen until I'm on the list for at least four years. Another year to wait!

December 1, 2010

I stop at the dialysis clinic this morning for an exchange then Maryellen follows me back to my house for a home visit.

I'm not feeling confident at all. The steps for the procedure are just not meshing completely in my mind. Thankfully, Don is with me, so whatever I forget, maybe he'll remember.

We're supposed to go to the annual Transplant Services Christmas party tonight, but my heart just isn't in it. Knowing I will have to come home and hook up for my first full night of dialysis petrifies me. And this would certainly spoil the party for us, so we stay at home. Maybe next year.

December 2, 2010

I'm not feeling well. I have no appetite and my weight is going up. I thought with dialysis, your weight should come down. I call Maryellen and she changes the formula. We try the cycler again tonight, and it was a nightmare. We turn it off.

My PD catheter site is not healing. It looks angry and red. I stop the antibiotic cream, Bactroban, and simply start a cream that Don has — a triple-antibiotic cream from the local drug store. Maryellen thinks I may be allergic to something in the Bactroban. Slowly, the PD catheter site clears up, and I am so thankful.

December 3, 2010

I continue to feel terrible. My sleep is so disrupted from the light and the noise of the cycler machine, and I still have the PD catheter pain. Sleeping is difficult in general. I can no longer lie on my stomach because of the tubing that protrudes. I sleep mostly on my back and occasionally on my side. I support the tubing while sleeping by simply holding on to it and giving it some slack so as not to cause a kink. If kinking occurs, the machine's alarm goes off and

I'm awakened and reminded to straighten the tubing so the liquid can flow in and out.

December 4, 2010

   My weight is now up about eight pounds and it's difficult sleeping again tonight. I'm having trouble breathing. We call Bethany, the dialysis nurse on call, four times, and finally get a return call at 3 a.m. She wants to meet us at the dialysis clinic today at 9 a.m. That hour can't come soon enough.

December 5, 2010

   We meet with Bethany at the dialysis clinic at 9 a.m. Apparently, she only received our fourth and last phone page. She calls the paging company and reports the problem to them.

   She shows Don how to do a manual exchange, as he was not present when I learned this in my class. This is helpful to him, but when we get home, we discover we don't have the "Stay Safe" bags necessary to do the exchange. They were never delivered to our home. Bethany finds some extra bags at the clinic and brings them to our home. This certainly isn't going smoothly for us.

   I can't eat and I feel poorly. I feel worse now than before I began dialysis. My weight is up ten pounds. Why is this? I just don't know. If I'm retaining fluid, which I don't believe I am, this fluid should be removed during dialysis. In general, fluid is put into the abdominal cavity, and fluid and toxins come out.

December 6, 2010

   Maryellen is back at work from her weekend away and calls me. I update her, although I believe Bethany already has. We change the formula again. I'm to do three manual exchanges today. I'm becoming quite the expert with manual exchanges. It's getting a lot easier for me to do, too. I guess practice really does make perfect.

December 7, 2010

I wake up, still not feeling well at all. My chest is hurting and I feel full of fluid. Maryellen asks me to come to the clinic and I do. My lungs are clear. Don and I are going to try the cycler again tonight — with yet another formula.

Each color bag of dialysate solutions represents a different percentage of dialysis fluid. Some are stronger than others at removing fluids. It's important to use the right dialysate solution for my needs or it may pull too much or too little fluid out of my body, or cause low blood pressure, swelling, or muscle cramping. Every day I weigh myself, and based on that weight, I know which bag to use.

December 8, 2010

I wake up after a fairly full night's rest and I'm feeling wonderful. It's 8 a.m. About an hour into my morning, I start to get short of breath and my pulse increases. I call Maryellen and she wants me to manually drain, but only put 500 mL into my abdominal cavity for the rest of the day instead of the usual 800 mL. That makes sense to me. I'm thinking that I may be getting way too much fluid for someone my size.

Maryellen tells me my labs are in and my hemoglobin is now down to 10.5 g. That's low, especially for someone as active as I'm still trying to be. She wants me to stop at the clinic tomorrow for an injection of Aranesp. I'm exhausted now, so at 9:30 a.m., I go back to bed for another two hours. Later this evening, I change the numbers on the cycler again and hope for a better night and a better tomorrow.

Because I've had some cycler problems, a new cycler machine is ordered for me. This one works much better. My formula seems to be correct now and I think I'm finally on my way. It has been a very rough start, but I'm amazed at how well I can now manage the program. I begin to feel much better and am no longer intimidated by the machine. My confidence grows.

I know some patients who have been on dialysis for a good many years. Hmm…I wonder how long I'm going to be on dialysis.

CHAPTER 11

Reactions From Friends

IF YOU ARE at the point in your journey where your family and friends have just learned of your health situation, then you can relate well to this chapter.

October 20, 2010

I meet a dear friend, Bea B., for lunch today. Bea had been my hairdresser for many years until she retired. We lost contact for about four years, during which time she had had a double mastectomy. We have a wonderful lunch and visit, just catching up. I e-mail her when I got home to express the joy of seeing her again.

She replies by saying:

"You know the old saying, Carole, 'Make new friends, but keep the old; new ones are silver, the old ones are gold.' It was great seeing you again. I was thinking on the way home just how much stress you are under. With my surgery, everything moved so fast. From diagnosis to surgery was only two weeks. I had little time to think about it. My heart goes out to you my brave, brave friend. God Bless. XOXO"

October 24, 2010

We're in Bethlehem this weekend, and I think I should probably e-mail a few friends to let them know I'm now on dialysis. I can certainly use their support. One person I decide to e-mail is Tammy McClenaghan from the Pennsylvania Governor's Residence, where I have been a docent since 2001. She is the Residence Manager and in charge of docent scheduling. I don't believe she knows anything about my health problems. I look forward to hearing back from her.

October 25, 2010: Tammy's response:

"Aww, Carole, I had no idea you were dealing with this. I'm so sorry Jay wasn't a match; it must have been a huge disappointment for her also, but she's given you the opportunity to expand to the Paired Donor Transplant List, which will certainly increase your chances of finding a match. How common is O Positive blood type? I'm A Negative, but I'm not sure how that all works as to which would be the most common or the rarest. I'm hoping O Positive is a more common type, thus increasing your chances for a donor.

"You've hidden this well, my friend… you'll be in my prayers. Carole, I can't imagine what you must be going through right now. I've never heard of home dialysis. Is that something that has to be done several days a week? Daily? Is it painful? I have so many questions, I know so very little about kidney disease and dialysis, while I'm sure you're quickly becoming an expert (although not by choice). Please let me know if there is anything I can do to help you as you go through this. Would you like me to share this with the docents — it would certainly increase your prayer circle?

"Please know you're in my thoughts, and I will pray that it won't be much longer until a match is found for you. Again, please let me know what I can do to help. In love and friendship, Tammy"

October 28, 2010

Today, I sent an e-mail to my fellow Soroptimists. The Soroptimist organization is a women's service organization meaning "Women Helping Women" and I have been a member for over 14 years. We do a lot of good work locally, as well as nationally and internationally, helping both women and girls in many negative situations.

"Hello Everyone,

"I would like to share something with you. On November 30, 2007, I was placed on the National Kidney Transplant List. As a result of a birth defect, I have deteriorating kidney disease. A young woman friend of mine (Jeanette) has offered to give me her kidney; however, after being tested, we learned that we do not match. Her blood type is AB (and she can donate to an A, a B, or an AB, but not an O). I am an O and can only receive a kidney from someone with an O blood type. However, her generosity has allowed me to now be placed on the Paired Donor List. Jeanette's kidney may go to someone in another area and my new kidney may come from someone in another area, wherever they can find a match.

"I thought I may have about another six months of good health, but things are happening quickly, and I have been very sick for the past month. It is now suggested that I go on home dialysis. I will have surgery next Thursday, November 4, for catheter placement, and then will be trained to do home dialysis daily. Hopefully, a new kidney will some day be forthcoming. My blood type makes the search more difficult. Please keep me in your prayers. That's so important to me. God's blessings to you all. Carole"

I got many answers and here are just a few:

"Carole, I read your message regarding your physical condition around 10 p.m. last Thurs. night. I was so upset, I called Helen P. and got her out of bed. We were to leave the next morning for Butler, PA, so I assumed she would be awake. I have thought about you and prayed a lot since reading your e-mail. I have known for some time something was wrong. Particularly, when I asked you to consider running for VP and you told me "perhaps next year." I did not ask what was wrong, as I assumed it was personal to you and you alone, but I did worry. If there is anything concrete that I can do for you such as doctors' apts., tests, etc., please let me know. I have no responsibilities at home and am very flexible. Love ya, Sally"

"Carole, I am so disheartened that you are having this problem. I know that we have often talked about this, but you always hope and pray that it will never happen. I feel worse than you can possibly imagine, but I know you and your determination and know that things will work out on your behalf. You have what it takes, my friend, and always come out a winner, in no matter what endeavor confronts you, and this will be no different. I just wish that I lived closer to you to help you in whatever manner I could, even to just make you a pot of soup. Please take good care of yourself, slow down, and concentrate on you, nothing else. Love, Sheila"

"Whatever the future holds, you can count on me to be there for you whenever I am needed. You have been my buddy for a long time and I will stand by for your call. Love Always, Doris"

November 16, 2010

Because my appetite is so poor, I rationalize that eating anything is better than eating nothing at all, so I eat my favorites. And steak sandwiches are definitely one of my very favorite foods!

One day as I was standing in line at a small restaurant, waiting to order a steak sandwich, I heard someone say, 'Why, hello, Carole! How are you?" I turned around and saw Rev. Keith Eslinger, Don's pastor from St. Timothy's Lutheran Church in Camp Hill, PA. I automatically responded, "Oh, hi, Pastor Keith. I'm just fine, thank you." And then I hesitated and thought about it, and replied, "Actually, no, I'm really not fine. In fact, I'm not doing well at all. My kidneys are failing and I'm facing dialysis. It's been a really difficult time for me." The smile left his face and he just listened while I continued talking, the words tumbling out of my mouth. I just couldn't stop them. Finally, he simply asked, "Would you mind if I put you on our prayer list?" "Oh, please do," I said, "please. I'd appreciate any and all prayers that would be said for me." It was such a comfort talking to him and I felt so much better after our conversation.

Before my journey ended, I would knowingly be on a total of seven prayer lists. Simply realizing this proved to be a great source of comfort and strength for me.

CHAPTER 12

The Patient and Family Partner Program®

Maryellen had told me that my local kidney foundation, The Kidney Foundation of Central PA (KFCP), had a Patient and Family Partner Program (PFPP). This is a nationally recognized mentoring program that trains and certifies medically stable dialysis patients and their caregivers and pairs them with newly diagnosed patients and their caregivers. Well-established mentoring programs are available for breast cancer and hospice patients, but PFPP is the only program of its kind that exists in the nation for people with kidney disease.

In 2004, after a year of curriculum development by 15 medical professionals, social workers and patients, KFCP launched PFPP as a pilot project in the greater Harrisburg area. This program has expanded to all of central Pennsylvania since that time.

Currently, there are 65 certified trained partners locally who have mentored over 100 patients. Simply put, mentors befriend patients, answer some of their nonmedical questions, and are there for them in an encouraging and supportive role. KFCP trains their mentors in an eight-week program, two hours per week. They ask that each mentor contact their mentee weekly and become involved with them as a support person for a period of three months to one year.

Just what I needed! Where do I sign up? This would give me additional emotional support in this area, as most of my close friends are in Bethlehem. I filled out the application and waited to be matched.

January 27, 2011

Michelle Mullikin calls me and introduces herself as my partner in PFPP. I've been connected! How wonderful is that! She is traveling for work and calls me from an airport. We have a great conversation and begin to share our stories.

Michelle said she received her new kidney about five years ago from a young man, but her story is involved and quite sad. One day, she and an acquaintance reported to Transplant Services at Harrisburg Hospital for their evaluation. Michelle had recently seen her OB/GYN and had had some tests done. Dr. Yang had those test results and came into the room to discuss them with her. He broke the terrible news to her that one of the tests revealed rectal cancer and she needed surgery. The Tumor Board at Harrisburg Hospital said she would also need to wait two years to receive a new kidney. The cancer had to be resolved before they could proceed with the transplant. Such devastating news! I can't imagine how difficult that moment in time must have been for her.

Her prospective donor went ahead with her own tests, and a chest x-ray revealed spots on her lungs. The spots were not diagnosed as cancer, but she did require medical care. She considers herself lucky to have had the chest x-ray; otherwise, who knows when the spots may have been discovered.

After her two-year wait, Michelle's first kidney offer came when she was working in Ohio. She drove back 6-½ hours in pouring-down rain, but didn't receive the kidney. There were several other patients on the list ahead of her. Shortly thereafter, she received another phone call, and this kidney was meant to be hers. She received the transplant and today she's doing just fine. I so admire this woman, and if ever I become discouraged, I think of her story and remember her grace and strength.

Michelle knows firsthand what I'm experiencing. To know someone who has actually walked the same path I'm walking now is of enormous benefit to me. Family and friends cannot possibly relate to what I'm going through, try as they might, not as well as someone who has actually been through it themselves. Together, we share the understanding of such a journey.

Michelle said she would call me again and that I should feel free to call her, but we should also keep in touch through e-mails. I look forward to doing both.

I believe PFPP should be available nationwide. It is so worthwhile. If it's not in your area, talk with the director of your local kidney foundation. Express an interest in bringing this program to your state. Refer to the *Resources* section of this book to get more information, including startup information for such a program.

CHAPTER 13

Kidney Offers

WAITING FOR A kidney is a little like waiting for a fire alarm to sound. Don and I never knew when a call would come through — a call that said a kidney was available for *me*. We worked out the details — transportation, notifying family, putting the business on hold, etc. Always, always, we needed to be prepared.

December 16, 2010, 7:15 a.m.

I'm sleeping in this morning, simply because I can, when the phone rings. I'm thinking it's earlier in the morning than what it is and that Don will certainly answer it. He gets up every morning around 4 a.m. It rings and rings. The answering machine clicks on just as I pick up the phone. It's Madeline with a kidney call! Oh, dear God, I can't believe it! Although just a backup kidney call, it is nevertheless a kidney call. She asks me, "Are you healthy? Did you have recent surgery? Any recent transfusions?" I guess it can be said that I'm healthy, but I'm certainly not feeling well.

No, no recent surgeries, no transfusions. Madeline said the computer spat out my name for a deceased kidney and the nephrologist on call said it was okay to call me. I can't believe this system is really working for me. I call for Don, who is in the lower level of our home and can't hear me. I can hardly wait to tell him!

Madeline tells me to take my morning pills with a minimum amount of water and to wait for a phone call from her in several hours. I hang up the phone and kneel down and pray. I tell Don the good news when he comes into the bedroom and together we pray again. What a day this is going to be...will it indeed be my lucky day?

Thoughts race through my mind and I remember just last evening when I was listening to Glenn Beck on his TV talk show. He spoke about the importance of "believing and expecting miracles." Right then, I said out loud and with confidence, "I believe I will get a new kidney. It will be a miracle and I don't know when, but I WILL get a new kidney." Now whether or not it happens today, I don't know, but I'm going to continue to be positive and to believe. Isn't that something? Just when I take on a forceful, positive attitude.

Some days I worried about the surgery itself and whether or not the new kidney would work when it was placed in me. These thoughts overwhelmed me. I reminded myself that God was with me and would walk with me every step of the way; and if for some reason, I didn't make it, then I would walk with Him.

Strange, but throughout this entire journey, I never really thought I would die. During all my conversations with God, He never prepared me by telling me that I might not make it. He spared me a lot of worry. So I was always optimistic and felt that this was something I would be able to get through with good results.

At 10:30 a.m., Madeline calls me again and tells me that I'm now second in line for the kidney, first backup. She had called other patients on the list, but they were not well enough to be considered. We had one hour to get to Harrisburg Hospital. I told Madeline that I just needed to wash my bathrobe first, and we laughed. She said, "Just go, you don't need to wash your robe," but I knew I did. And so I did.

Don drives me to Harrisburg Hospital. We each have our own thoughts, feeling both excited and anxious. I'm admitted at noon and go to the 6th floor, the surgical floor. I have 14 vials of blood drawn for tests, including a final cross-match to ensure that I'm compatible with the available organ. An EKG is performed and an IV is started.

Don decides to call Father Tim to let him know we are settled in my room and he could now visit me. The cell phone doesn't work too well in the room, so Don takes the elevator down to the outside of the hospital and makes the call.

In the meantime, Dr. Narins comes in to talk to me. He tells me about the deceased donor. He was a 25-year-old man who had problems with depression and shot himself in the head. Dr. Narins doesn't know his tissue type yet, but the body is expected to go into surgery soon. At that time, the organs will be viewed to check for viability of harvesting, and of course, the deceased will be tissue typed. Dr. Narins assures me that if he doesn't return to tell me, "Merry Christmas, you got the kidney," I will get a kidney. He was quite serious and I knew he meant it. I am so encouraged.

Father Tim comes into my room. He anoints me and prays with us. I so need and appreciate his visit.

And then we wait, and we wait. I have had nothing to eat since the evening before, and no water since this morning. Finally, at 9:30 p.m., my nurse brings a cell phone to me, and it is Madeline on the line. She tells me that the man ahead of me got the kidney, only because he had seniority on the transplant list. He matched, and I matched as well. Imagine that! Their decision is a sad one for me, but I bet it's a very happy one for the man. I learn he's from the Philadelphia area, the same area as the deceased. I also learn that patients are often called into the hospital for a potential transplant several times before they actually receive one. Can this be just the first of many times for me?

It was a very long day for us. And what a roller coaster ride we had been on! Don and I were totally exhausted, both physically and emotionally. But now we knew the system worked and we truly felt that we had just come through a small miracle. Yes, we were disappointed I didn't get the kidney, but there was nothing more I could have done. Rules are rules and you learn that in this long process they were made for a reason and must be adhered to. If the man was on the transplant list longer than I and we both matched, then he deserved to get the kidney. I simply understood that.

I am so-o hungry after we leave the hospital. We stop at Perkins to get something to eat. It's 9:50 p.m., and they close at 10 p.m. I quickly order a club sandwich and really enjoy drinking and drinking the water. Home we go...to get some rest and to recuperate.

I still faced taking a 45-passenger bus to Bethlehem in less than two days. This bus trip was a fundraiser for Soroptimist and I was in charge of it. I had set up the itinerary and completely planned the day about two months ago. But only by the grace of God will I ever be able to do this. The hospital stay set me back all the more — no food or water for such a long period of time. A part of me wondered if I was even physically fit for transplant surgery. I had not been eating or sleeping well at all. Well, maybe that was why God chose the man ahead of me to get the new kidney. Everything happens for a reason.

December 18, 2010

I'm up very early today to meet the bus and greet the people before they board. And off to Bethlehem we go at 7:30 a.m. I can't believe I'm even able to do this — only with God's help. The day goes well and everyone seems to enjoy the festiveness of this little Christmas town. Being in charge of a bus trip is a lot of responsibility — helping everyone enjoy their day and leaving no one behind — but I did it. We are back in the parking lot at the scheduled 8 p.m. time, and I arrive home completely exhausted.

December 19, 2010

I look down at my ankles and feet and see that both legs are swollen. This is a first for me and I'm sure it's a bad sign. I call Maryellen and she recommends stronger dialysis solution. She also wants me to add another cycle, Cycle #7, to my nightly regimen. This way, I will be getting more dialysis. I can do that, but I will then be on the cycler for ten hours every night.

It took three days for the swelling to go down, the left leg being worse than the right. It was nice to see my "real" feet again. I wondered why this happened. I had chicken noodle soup at the restaurant over the weekend and it was very salty. I hoped it was simply what I ate and that the swelling would not recur again in the future and become a permanent problem.

December 25, 2010

Christmas! I'm beginning to feel a little better. My skin appears less yellow/grey. I've had three injections for my anemia, so I'm sure my hemoglobin has improved. My appetite is good, and I'm finally sleeping fairly well. What more can I ask? I'm really quite happy with all the improvements and look forward to feeling even better in the future as the dialysis continues. It's a good holiday for me.

Should a new kidney offer come along now, I believe I'll be healthy enough to get through the surgery. And that's a very good thing! I'm physically stronger today than I was when I received my first kidney offer. And facing a possible transplant now does not seem so overwhelming to me.

December 31, 2010

Don and I return to our Mechanicsburg home, having spent our usual week between Christmas and New Year's in our Bethlehem house. We check our answering machine for messages and play them all back. One is from Betty H., a woman from Don's church. Apparently, Pastor Keith wrote a short article for the church's newsletter about me needing a kidney. Betty read it and was calling to say she would like to be my donor. She is O positive and had been willing to donate to her sister in the fall of 2010, but the doctors at Hershey Medical Center deemed her sister a noncandidate because of her heart problems. One glitch, however, may be that Betty is 69 years old. She certainly doesn't look her age. She claims to be in excellent health, exercises three times a week, and is on no medication. Also, her mother is 95 years old and doing just fine. But can you imagine? A stranger wanting to donate to me.

I believe Harrisburg Hospital is more stringent with their donor rules than most transplant centers. It's Friday afternoon and I give Betty Jeri's phone number nevertheless. Betty calls Jeri and leaves a message. It will be a long weekend.

I am in awe, just total disbelief. I never, ever expected this kind of response from St. Timothy's newsletter. God sure works in mysterious ways. I hope the news from Jeri will either be very good or very bad (like we're a good tissue match or not.) I hate to have the decision rest totally on me for a kidney of that age. I just wouldn't know what to do.

January 4, 2011

I receive a call from Jeri, telling me that Betty had not been accepted because of her age. PinnacleHealth Transplant Services' age limit is 65 years of age, and Betty is 69. She said Betty really wanted to donate and thought it would be her decision alone to make. Fortunately or not, that's not the case. Rules are made for a reason. So that ends that. My second kidney offer isn't going to materialize. I wonder what lies ahead...

January 7, 2011

Jay calls me from her home in Pittsburgh. I congratulate her on her recent marriage. It took place out of the country between Christmas and New Year's. She is now Jay

Diaz-Tolin. She tells me she just received a call from Jeri. Jeri told her they wanted her kidney in the Paired Donor Program and that they had a kidney for me. Wow! I never expected to hear that. We matched two other women from the Pittsburgh area. Jeri was sending Jay blood tubes for a Monday blood draw, and Jay was to send them back to her via Overnight Express. Is this really happening?

About 5:30 p.m. today, I get a call from Madeline. She tells me basically the same thing Jay has just told me. Madeline wants me at Transplant Services next Tuesday for a fresh blood draw. I'm getting really excited now…until I tell her that I'm scheduled for foot surgery for plantar fasciitis on Friday, January 14. It will be minor, out-patient surgery involving the partial cutting of the fascia in the sole of my foot for freer movement. The surgery date had been set in the fall of 2010 because January is a slow time of the year for my business. Madeline wonders if this will affect my eligibility. She said she will look into it and get back to me.

January 9, 2011

Don and I go to St. Timothy's 10:30 a.m. church service with the hopes of meeting this generous woman who offered to donate her kidney to me. When we "pass the peace," Betty comes over to us. She shakes Don's hand and then gives me a big hug. I am so happy to actually meet her, and I sincerely thank her. It takes a very special person to be a kidney donor, so I want to send her a written thank-you note as well.

As Don and I walk out of church, Pastor Keith greets us and immediately proceeds to tell us about another woman in the congregation who wants to donate her kidney to me. She is 40 years old, so age will not be a problem. He believes she will be contacting me soon. Tears fill my eyes, and once again, I am in disbelief.

When we got home, I wrote Betty this thank-you note —

"Dear Betty,

"It was great to actually meet you today! What a very special person you are. I had to send you this written "thank-you" note for your unselfish kidney offer.

"Don said you're one of God's precious angels, and I must emphatically agree. I simply cannot get over your generosity and thank God so often for your kindness. Our paths crossed for some reason, and if at any time in the future you are in need of anything, please don't hesitate to call on me. I will always feel a special bond toward you, Betty.

"Best wishes for a happy, healthy 2011, filled with many dreams come true. May God bless you and keep you in His care. Carole"

January 11, 2011

Don and I go to Transplant Services to have my blood drawn again. I thought it might be something more, like meeting with the surgeon, too, but no, just a fresh blood sample for testing.

January 14, 2011

I have foot surgery for my plantar fasciitis. Nothing major, but now the kidney transplant surgery can't be scheduled until February. With the Paired Donor List, we all learn of our surgery date well before the surgery. Very convenient! Transplant Services wants my foot to heal completely before I go on immunosuppressive drugs. These drugs delay healing, so it's important that I go ahead with the surgery and get it behind me.

I spend the next entire week at home, elevating and icing my foot for 50 minutes out of every hour. It made for a very long week indeed, but my foot healed well.

January 25, 2011

Today, I learn that my kidney donor is 64 years old. Hmmm, now I'm wondering... She is so close to the maximum age of 65. Her GFR is 95 with the average being 85. That's a good thing, of course, but now I have some concerns. I call Jeri to see what her thoughts are about this. I also call Maryellen. They both feel this is an "on-the-fence" kind of offer and that I need to get more information and possibly some reassurance.

I call Dr. Diamond's office. His assistant gets back to me, "Dr. Diamond said that it's a good kidney if it has a GFR of over 100." My kidney offer is 95. Possibly another reason to inquire further.

January 27, 2011

I talk to Michelle and tell her that I have received a kidney offer through the Paired Donor Program and that my donor is 64 years old. What are her thoughts on this? She said she would have concerns, too. She suggests that I speak to Dr. Yang, and if Dr. Yang thinks it's "a good kidney," it is indeed "a good kidney." This seems like sound advice. I call Madeline and ask for an appointment to speak with Dr. Yang; she tells us to come in the next day.

January 28, 2011

Don and I go to Transplant Services and meet with Dr. Yang. It is Dr. Yang's opinion right from the start that this is a good kidney for me. (I believe he means for my age.) He said I would only get a kidney from an age 60+ pool unless I found a younger donor. He gives me no wiggle room, so I decide right then and there to accept this offer. I forget to tell him about my 69-year-old donor, but I did mention about the second woman (age 40) from St. Timothy's who's in the wings. He said, of course, that would be a better kidney, but she hasn't been approved yet and anything can happen between the time she's actually tested and signs on the dotted line. I'm afraid to take the chance. Also, if I decline this offer, the surgery will be called off for the other recipient as well, and I feel a certain responsibility for her. I believe God has led me to this point for a reason, and this is His choice for me as well. An important reason to go ahead with this offer.

When I get home, I e-mail Jay to let her know I have accepted this kidney offer. She doesn't get back to me right away, which is rather unusual, so I call her later in the evening. Sadly, she tells me she lost her job that day. She is very upset. Apparently, the company she worked for had purchased three other companies and subsequently elimi-nated the marketing department, which she was part of. I'm so sorry to hear this. It certainly makes for an unstable time for her. Hmmm…I wonder what this might do to Jay's plans to donate her kidney.

The week of February 1 was rather stressful for me, as a surgery date had not yet been confirmed. One phone call from Jay led me to believe that it may be March 9. Oh, dear, I certainly hope not. I really didn't feel well at all — and that's just rather long to wait. Finally, I get a call from Madeline and she informed me that the date of February 21 had just been finalized, and that was enough time to allow my foot to heal completely. Madeline made an appointment for me at Transplant Services for Wednesday, February 16, to get my final instructions, a blood draw, a chest x-ray, and an EKG. Don and I will also be meeting with the surgeon and financial coordinator. It will be another long, involved day.

February 14, 2011

*I wake up with the beginnings of a deep cough and the start of a cold. I simply can't believe this! If I get a cold, all surgeries will have to be cancelled. **Please, God, please no. I have come this far; let me conclude with the surgery on Monday.** I call Madeline to see if she wants to put me on any medication. She said I needed to call my family doctor or Dr. Diamond. I call Dr. Diamond, but it's clinic day, so I just go to the drug store and buy Robitussin Cough and Cold medicine. It quiets the cough, but like most cough medications, it affects my bowels. I continue to drink prune juice (not knowing it was full of potassium). I also use a nasal spray frequently, hoping to ward off the cold. If it isn't one thing, it's another.*

February 16, 2011

Don and I have a 4-hour appointment at Transplant Services. I sign a number of papers giving consent, etc., and meet with Jeri, as Madeline is on vacation. Jeri explains everything to us and in detail. We meet with Dr. Yang again, who says I should be excited, not worried, as they know what they're doing and have done it many times before. He sounds so reassuring. We meet with our financial coordinator, but don't really learn anything new. We would like to know exactly what our expenses are going to be. Since I'm on Medicare, I believe most of my expenses will be covered. I guess we'll just have to wait and see.

I'm told that transplant surgery for the recipient usually takes 2 to 3 hours with hospitalization generally between 5 to 7 days. Most patients go to the ICU for one day. Discharge happens when I'm medically stable and post-transplant teaching is complete.

I'm really tired today and barely able to think clearly. I'm not feeling well at all. My sleep habits have been awful — I don't sleep well on the cycler at night or for enough hours, so I wake up exhausted. I'll be so glad when I can lie on my stomach once again and not need the cycler. That time cannot come soon enough.

Dr. Yang offers me an opportunity to be part of a research drug program for a study medication, everolimus. Paula Kratzer, RN, BSN, CCTC, comes into our room and reads the ten-page consent form to us. She assures me that the drug has been approved both here and in Europe.

The purpose of any accepted research by Dr. Yang and his group is for the benefit of the patient. Dr. Yang believes that patients who are on this program do much better because they are followed more closely, and any problems that may occur are detected early on.

By agreeing to be on this program, the medication would be paid for, and I would receive $30 per doctor's visit. One big negative for me was that a kidney biopsy was mandatory in six months. I dreaded this, but I decided to go ahead and become part of the program in spite of it. Following surgery, an envelope would be opened and would reveal whether I was to be given the old drug

(CellCept) or the new drug (Everolimus). Everolimus is not toxic to the kidney. Research on this drug could lead to its greater use for other kidney patients.

Before I leave Transplant Services, Jeri tells me my name came up on the list that morning for a cadaver kidney. Unbelievable! That makes five kidney offers in two months — the cadaver kidney on December 16, the two women from Don's church, the Paired Donor offer (which I accepted), and now this second cadaver kidney offer. How lucky am I.

February 17, 2011
Jeri calls me and tells me my potassium level is up and the surgeons will not operate until I get it down. She tells me what diet to follow, but I believe it's the prune juice that's causing the problem, so I totally eliminate it.

Michelle and I meet for lunch. Finally, I can put a name to a face. How nice! With my surgery date set for Monday, February 21, I still have a number of questions. And she answers all of them. Over lunch, we continue to share our experiences and have such a wonderful time together. We hug in the parking lot and she wishes me well. She is such a great support person for me.

February 18, 2011
My blood is drawn and my potassium level is checked again. It's now normal and surgery is on.

February 20, 2011
It's one day before surgery and I am so-o ready. I'm still fighting a cold, but I hope and pray it is not apparent before surgery. I receive some phone calls and several e-mails from

friends, wishing me well. It's so nice to hear from them. I talk with Jay and thank her, again, and wish her good luck with her surgery. She tells me she really likes her surgeon, thinks he's "cool." I'm happy to hear that.

I bake some chocolate chip cookies for Jay and box them carefully for shipment in a Priority Mail box. I also wrap each of the small gifts I bought her for her recuperative period and include them in the box. I ask Don to mail it to her one day after our surgery.

Don was just informed that a tour of the Pentagon in Washington, DC, had been planned for Thursday, February 24. It's organized by his pilot friend, Mike, who is in the Air Force and stationed at the Pentagon. I knew Don really wanted to go. I encouraged him to do so, as I felt I would be just fine in the hospital.

Don e-mailed Mike regarding my surgery during that week, and Mike replied:

"Don, first off, thanks for the update...we've been praying for Carole for the last few months and I am glad to hear we can be cautiously optimistic about the future.... God is in charge, no matter what we think or feel about it. The procedure you described is nothing less than amazing to me...so many good people acting at once.... incredible. I would like to try to donate blood again...I did try two years ago and was banned in PA due to places I have lived and served...if there is a way to help in this regard, please let me know and I will try. Anything for you and Carole.

"Don, I totally understand about her, and possibly you, not being able to make the trip — if that happens, we can reschedule you a special trip — please let that be the least of your concerns this week. On the positive side, if you do make it, it will be great to see you. Hopefully you can get a plane ride.

"I will be praying especially hard on Monday...faith works miracles. MM"

CHAPTER 14

Transplant

MONDAY, FEBRUARY 21, 2011

Well, today is the day! I'm a little nervous and rather anxious as I face this huge challenge before me. Actually, there is no way to even prepare for an operation like this, but I am definitely ready. **Lord, I know you're with me.** *"The will of God will never take me where the grace of god will not protect me..." (author unknown).*

Don and I report to Outpatient Registration at Harrisburg Hospital at 5:30 a.m. I'm taken back to the pre-op area, where I change into my hospital gown. We're thinking it might be an early afternoon surgery, but what we didn't know is that Jay was told to be at the Starzl Institute at 4 a.m. for her surgery. So at 8:30 a.m., we're informed that the airplane has taken off from Pittsburgh with my new kidney, and it will be landing soon at Harrisburg Airport.

All of a sudden everything becomes a rush! An anesthesiologist comes in and asks me a lot of questions, the IV nurse starts my IV, and then off I go on my gurney to the OR. My abdomen is washed with a special soap and I'm given my first dose of immunosuppressive medications. This decreases my body's ability to fight off infections, but it's needed to prevent rejection of my new kidney. I know my transplant surgery will probably take between 2 to 4 hours and that my incision will be 6 to 8 inches long. The transplanted kidney will be hooked up to the main artery and vein that supplies blood flow to my right leg. It will also be connected to my bladder. I'm given some medication to relax me and that's all I remember.

The surgery went well and the new kidney performed beautifully. When I awoke in the RR less than two hours later, Dr. Yang leaned down toward my face and said, "It's pouring out," and laughed. Later, I was told that all you could see were my nose and eyes and you could hear me complaining that I was cold. The nurses put fluids into my IV to replace the urine output, but I guess it was hard to stay ahead of the kidney. Off now to the ICU, where Dr. Narins and Jeri informed me that I had indeed gotten a "good" kidney. The creatinine was 1.8 mg/dL. That's a great number! My creatinine was 5.5 mg/dL before surgery.

I'm given strong antirejection drugs. I had been made aware of their many side effects before surgery. I just didn't expect I would personally experience so many of them. My immune system is now depleted. Throughout my first night, I have problems with nausea and am given an antinausea medication, but then I can't connect my thoughts. My prayers are incomplete and I want so badly to thank God for helping me to get through the surgery. I can't get beyond a few simple phrases. My mind is looping, a side effect of the medicine, I'm told, and I have simply lost control.

Tuesday, February 22, 2011

Tuesday morning finally comes. It has been such a long, confusing night. My personal care assistant this morning is a young man, 19 years old, who places a tub of soapy water with a washcloth on my bed and says , "You can probably wash yourself." I had a Foley catheter in my bladder to measure urine output, a new 7-inch abdominal incision where the kidney was inserted, and a stent had been placed between my kidney and my bladder. I was on nasal oxygen, and I had an IV in my wrist. A PICC line had been inserted in my neck, extending into the large blood vessel in my chest for blood draws. It was really very difficult for me to wash myself. I asked him if he had had any training for this, and he said he had a few classes last year, but didn't really like the work. He wanted to be a firefighter or an EMT. I tried washing myself...

I arrive in my private room at about 10:45 a.m., still without breakfast or a decent bath. The day goes poorly. I need to get out of bed and walk to prevent post-op complications, such as blood clots and pneumonia. I walk to the bathroom for the first time and am shocked when I look in the mirror. My face is full and flushed. I don't even recognize myself. Where have I gone? I try combing my hair differently and washing my face again, but I'm not there. My spirit deflates. I have gained ten pounds of prednisone weight in about 24 hours and my balance is off. My feet are chubby and I have trouble walking. I cling to Don for support as we go for our first walk down the hall.

I now have higher blood sugars and am given insulin several times daily. I'm told this may just be "temporary diabetes" due to the high doses of prednisone, and hopefully, the diabetes will resolve when the dose is lowered. My blood sugars are checked four times daily with finger sticks. When my blood pressure goes up, extra medication is given.

I speak with Jay later this afternoon only to learn that she is being discharged to home, about 36 hours after her surgery. Good for her! She sounds a little groggy and she said she had some pain. I hope her discharge isn't too soon for her.

Wednesday, February 23, 2011

My first two nights have been awful. I'm on 200 mg of prednisone (a very high dose) and begin experiencing some side effects. I have a dull throbbing headache, but the medicine I need for relief cannot be given because it will injure the new kidney. My tremors stop soon enough, but now I experience mood swings. Happy one minute, crying the next. Nausea is controlled by a new antinausea medication that doesn't cause me any mental looping, but I barely sleep.

Prompt morning care and a good breakfast are a great way to begin my Wednesday. Dr. Narins comes in this morning and tells me about the stent that was placed between my kidney and my bladder to prevent the problem with reflux. This is good to hear. I would hate to experience the demise of a new kidney because of another reflux problem.

So much is totally out of my control during this hospitalization, but I can still control my responses to it all. And that's a good coping skill to know.

Father David visits me in the morning and Father Tim comes in the afternoon. I know I look my worst, but I welcome their prayers.

When Don visits me in the hospital today, he brings along a gift from a dear friend — a stuffed, handmade Lamb Chop. In 1957, ventriloquist Shari Lewis and her puppet friend, Lamb Chop, made their debut on television. Many of the nurses remember them. Lamb Chop gets a lot of attention and is a great source of comfort for me. Don tapes all my get-well cards to the bureau near my bed, and it certainly brightens up the room. Lots of good wishes from lots of good friends.

My wrist IV is discontinued and I feel so much better. The IV is moved to my PICC line. When it was inserted in the OR, a large dressing was applied so that my head and shoulder were closer together than comfortable, so I was unable to stand straight. This will be removed before discharge and I can hardly wait. Today, I am just so exhausted.

Finally, on night three, I experience some peaceful sleep, and it is simply medicinal.

Thursday, February 24, 2011

I am taken back to the OR at 8 a.m. today to have my PD catheter removed, as I no longer have any use for it. The prior incision paths are used, and I awake and my PD catheter is gone. I look at my belly and it reminds me of a series of railroad tracks, but except for the soreness and the Steri-Strips, it really doesn't bother me. I am grateful for so little pain.

I return to my room, where my personal care assistant now removes the Foley catheter. What a relief! I urinate about 200 mL on my very own and know that I am almost home free.

Dr. Diamond comes in to visit me and tells me that the Selection Committee had discussed the new kidney offer and believed it would be a good one for me, especially the size. That was good to know.

*Don and I attend several classes while in the hospital. Judy, a member of the post-transplant team arrives, and we are given a three-ring binder. We review all types of information and upcoming appointments. I know this team has educated **many** people before us. Judy gives me a large, four-doses-a-day pill box, and I fill it with medication that I must take daily, some for the rest of my life. I am on about 30 different pills currently, many of which are to trick my immune system into accepting the transplanted kidney. With time, I hope this number becomes less. I remember thinking I was on a lot of medicines when I was on about eight or nine pills a day. That's nothing compared to what I have to take now! I just swallow them down, many at a time, with a lot of water and never give it a second thought. It has to be done, so I best get used to it.*

Judy leaves, and a nurse comes in to give me instructions on diabetic care. She teaches me how to stick my finger for blood and how to use the small machine that will give me my daily blood sugar readings. So much to learn, and again, I am just so tired. It's very hard to concentrate.

Don left at 6 a.m. today for Washington, DC, so he could join the organized tour of the Pentagon. I was so glad he had the opportunity to do this.

Don visits me at the end of the day, and it is so good to see him. He brings me an artificial rose, since I can't have fresh flowers, and some cookies (now a no-no with my diabetes). What a man, he knows I love my sweets!

He's exhausted, so he goes home early. But I am just so glad he came and told me all about his exciting day in Washington.

Friday, February 25, 2011

It's Friday and today I'm hoping to be discharged. My teaching is complete, my immunosuppressive medications are available for me to take home, and my blood values are stable. The nurse removes my PICC line and takes out the tube and stitches. However, with this comes some skin tears, and I'm just hoping they will leave no scars. I am discharged late in the afternoon, just seven pounds over my regular weight, and am so anxious to get home.

Before discharge, I was told I could eat almost anything in moderation — including cantaloupe, tomatoes, orange juice, and dairy products. I was also told that I should never swim in a swimming pool; never take Advil, Aleve, or Motrin; never smoke; never eat grapefruit; never have birds or turtles as pets; and never get live vaccines. Just some of the rules for me to remember to follow. However, I would eventually be able to travel, return to work, exercise, and enjoy a fairly full life.

I am home now and I think about all that I have been through in one week. I'm sleeping in the comfort and safety of my own bed and slowly become overwhelmed with sadness. I start to cry…the tears finally coming, and I experience some much-needed relief. I feel my strength returning and know that God is in control and always has been. He never left me and only through His grace have I come through such a monumental week. I give Him all the credit…and always will. God is the physician of all physi-

cians. He guided the hands and minds of the surgeons and medical staff, and I thank Him profusely.

Finally, I am at peace with my situation. I know that with time I will be just fine and much of this past week will fade into memory.

CHAPTER 15

Post-Transplant

Now that I was home, I realized that responsibility for my health had shifted from medical personnel in the hospital to Don and me. The success of my recuperative period depended a lot more on me and those who cared about me. If you are a post-transplant patient, you may have experienced this same thinking.

Emotional support is paramount to any patient. I do believe, however, that today's fast-paced society has become rather insensitive and offhanded to those who are sick and suffering. I believe also that the medical profession cannot afford the luxury of just treating the patient's physical problems. I trust they will remember the importance emotions play, for only by treating the whole patient does complete healing occur.

February 26, 2011

Today, Saturday, is my first full day at home, and the phone rings off the hook. I try to talk with family and friends, but my voice is almost gone and what comes out is something like a croaking sound. Apparently, when my throat tube was removed following surgery, this became the result, but I was told my voice would improve in about six weeks. The callers are all so chipper and most comment, "You sound wonderful! Keep up the good work!" Now really…how can that possibly be?

I try to explain to those who call just how difficult it was for me in the hospital and the many reactions I had to the potent drugs, but no one seemed to listen. They just wanted to hear happy and positive things, but that would not be the truth. Yes, with time, I will be able to say that, but certainly not now. I become very frustrated and decide to take the phone off the hook.

I write my first article entitled, "One Week Post-op," and e-mail it to my family and friends, hoping to give them a better understanding of what I had actually been through this past week.

Some of the e-mails I received in response to that e-mail were:

"Carole, an emotional story of a gut-wrenching experience that no one else can possibly understand, but somehow we all begin to see and attempt to relate to the question we must ask ourselves: 'Could I have weathered this week that you speak of with such strength and grace?'

"You continue to amaze me with your beauty and honesty in words. Keep this going and then compile it to share with others… I think of you every day and don't want to interrupt the peace that you are beginning to experience. I will call tomorrow. Love, Diane"

"Wow, Carole. I, of course, had no idea. I'm glad you shared your experience thus far. And I will definitely keep praying and asking others to do the same. There's so much the rest of us don't understand. Janet"

"Carole, you brought tears to my eyes. I truly understand what you are going through. This brought back memories of my sister's transplant, and it is almost like she is writing for you. I can tell you this. Patti went through all you are saying, but she did it. It was never easy, but it did get easier. It is absolutely overwhelming for some time, but eventually it all makes sense. Yes, you will have a different lifestyle, but you will have a life. You are blessed to have a great husband in Don. Be strong and give yourself credit. You are a beautiful person inside and out and a lot of how you see yourself now is temporary. I know you can do this. Everyone is praying for you. Love, Nancy J."

"Carole, thank you so much for keeping me up to date about all that you've been through. My, I had no idea how grueling this process really is! It truly is 'suffering' that you have had to endure — physical, emotional and spiritual. It may certainly be true that our suffering, mysteriously, does bring us closer to Christ, but it doesn't always seem too comforting at the time to know this; it's more helpful on reflection. As I 'walked with you' through the letter you sent, please let me know how I might do that now. Christ be with you, and may you grow stronger in every way, day by day. Peace to you, Pastor Keith."

I am still diabetic and my blood pressures are quite high. The human body recovers slowly. I find it necessary to call the post-transplant person on call a few times during my first weekend home to get my medications adjusted. I listen to everything they tell me to do because this is all so overwhelming for me. I plan to dot every "i" and cross every "t" along this recuperative journey, as I don't want to do anything wrong that would jeopardize my new kidney. I'm probably one of their most compliant patients.

I thank God for Don, my caregiver, who is just so solid, attentive and caring. I doubt that we as patients can ever give enough credit to our caregivers, whoever they may be. When we have a good caregiver, our recovery is spontaneously hastened and enhanced. Patients simply couldn't get better without them.

Every ounce of my energy was focused on getting well. All I seemed to want to do was eat and sleep. I was told that eating three good meals a day would help the healing process, so that's exactly what I did. In addition, I ate two snacks — one around 3 p.m. and one before bed. I didn't gain any weight, which boggled my mind, as I knew I was really consuming calories. I watched what I ate because I was now on a diabetic diet. I had a pamphlet that guided me to the foods and portions that wouldn't raise my blood sugar. Also, I bought sugar-free puddings and ice cream. It was all quite manageable. But that was my concern…all I was doing was managing me, nothing more. For a very active person with a Type A personality to slow down mentally to this pace was all extremely challenging, but I was too physically sick to do otherwise. I have always been amazed at the resiliency of patients who are very ill. Now I guess I'm one of them and have a much clearer understanding of their trials. I believe God makes us strong when we need to be. He did so with me.

The first week home was very trying. To ensure success of the transplant, there were several expectations I had to meet. I needed to return to Transplant Services for care and management on a routine basis and as requested for urgent issues. Blood draws needed to be done twice a week for the first six months, declining with time. Medications needed to be taken three times a day. Vital signs were taken daily — my weight once a day, my blood pressures and blood sugars three times day, and my temperature twice a day. And it all had to be recorded in a log book. This log book went along with me to all my clinic appointments for review by the medical staff. I wasn't allowed to drive for two weeks after surgery, nor was I permitted to lift anything greater than 20 pounds for 4 to 6 weeks after surgery.

Because it was such a strain for me to talk, I often resorted to e-mail. That way, when I got tired, I just stopped writing. I got so many wonderful and encouraging messages. Of course, Don and I didn't allow visitors into our home because I was in my own "bubble" and would be so for about the next month.

With a depleted immune system, I had to wear my mask when I went to the lab for blood draws or to the doctor's office. I wasn't allowed flowers because spores or bacteria might be on them, and I needed to guard against infections at all costs. However, I did get one arrangement. I was honestly quite happy to see it, as I so love flowers. I wore my mask when I looked at the bouquet close up, but then Don tucked it away in the lower level of our home. I also wasn't allowed fresh fruit with skins on, also because of bacteria. I had to scrub the skins well, or simply not eat them. I did receive an Edible Arrangement, and wow! that fresh fruit was fantastic. That I could eat. I was so excited when the Edible Arrangements truck pulled up to our home, just like on TV. What a thoughtful gift.

I so appreciated the family and friends who brought food to Don and me. I never realized the true value of doing this until now. Don did all the cooking, so it was a relief for him to skip a day or two. And we got to try some wonderful recipes as well. Don's parents, Harrison and Marvel, are the best cooks and brought us great homemade food. Everything was so fresh and tasty. And their pies! I love the Thanksgiving holidays and their contributions of homemade pies, the best I've ever tasted.

Cards poured in, and the highlight of my day was when the mailman delivered mail. I often wished he'd deliver mail on Sundays, too. I received a total of 186 cards. That seemed like an awful lot to me, as I had very few family members still alive. However, Don and I do know a lot of people through our businesses, community work and organizations. People were so kind. I read their cards frequently and was uplifted and grateful each and every time. Reading cards over and over again made me feel remembered and cared for.

I missed Brandie so very much. Her passing came at such a distressing time for me. Were she here, I would have derived a lot of satisfaction from just talking, petting and simply loving her. She would have been a great comfort to me. It's true that pets help in the healing process. But unfortunately, I couldn't turn back the hands of time, so all I had were memories.

My day revolved around the clock. My morning monitoring began at 8 a.m. by taking a handful of medications. Usually I was at my worst about an hour or so after I took the medicines. My pulse went up and I was just extremely tired and needed to sleep. That improved as the day went on. I checked another blood sugar reading at noontime and enjoyed a big lunch. At 5 p.m., I did my routine checks again, and then had dinner. At 8 p.m., I took more medications, and then it was almost time for bed. Come morning, I repeated the entire process again.

February 28, 2011
   Don and I report to Transplant Services for my first appointment following surgery. We meet with Dr. Yang; Mary Waybill, MD, my research/transplant nephrologist;

Brandie hopes for a treat.

Carole shows Brandie's retractable leash to
grandchildren Cheyenne and Grayson Fair.

*and Paula. I have my blood drawn to check drug levels, in
addition to other tests, and give a urine sample.*

Paula and I would talk frequently during my first year
postop. I relied on her medical expertise (along with advice
from Dr. Waybill) to guide me on what medication doses
to take, when to stop certain medicines, and to setup timely
clinic appointments. She was my lifeline during this time,
so dependable and always only a phone call away.

*Everyone is so glad to see me and comment on how well I
look. They can't get over that I'm not wearing a sweat suit.
"You just had surgery! You're usually swollen and then with
the added prednisone weight …and you're wearing your
regular jeans!" My weight is just about back to normal, but*

I am far from feeling well. However, their kind words boost my spirits and brighten my day. Bless them!

Dr. Yang comments, "You're doing excellently. You're just one week after surgery!" I tell him that I will take very good care of my new kidney, and he says, "I know you will." I want to become one of their good statistics. Receiving a kidney transplant is a very precious gift, but with it comes a lot of personal responsibility.

March 3, 2011

Today, I have my first appointment with the endocrinologist who will treat me for my diabetes. My blood sugars are still a bit high, so it's very important that I continue to monitor them, adhere to my diet, and take my medications.

Every Monday and Thursday morning for the next six months, I will have blood drawn, mainly to check that the antirejection drugs are within the range they need to be. I hope my veins hold out. I can actually feel the scar tissue when the technician sticks the needle into my veins, and entry into my veins become a little more difficult with each visit to the lab.

March 7, 2011

I have an appointment with a urologist today. The stent that was placed between my kidney and my bladder during my transplant surgery now has to be removed. The doctor removes the stent and I ask if I can take it home as a souvenir. Sure, he says. The procedure is uncomfortable, but not painful. I can now eliminate one of my antibiotics.

March 8, 2011

It's been two weeks since my surgery, and I have now been given permission to drive. I want to go out into soci-

ety, but I really don't know where to go. It's either to the library or to Wegmans for a piece of pizza. The latter wins out. I love pizza! I couldn't eat any when I had ESRD. It's only 11 a.m. when I drive to Wegmans, about three miles from our home, just to eat pizza. I come home totally exhausted and sleep for two hours. But I am elated at this small accomplishment...and the pizza tasted great.

March 12, 2011

Don debuts Apollo 18 today at the Alpaca Owners & Breeders Assn. show in York, PA. I can't go and am very disappointed. I'm still in my "bubble" and can't risk being with so many people and so many animals. Don took over the training of Apollo 18 in January, as I was too sick to

Don and Carole with their extended family:
Apollo 18, Julianna and Brynia.

Apollo 18 takes 2nd place at PAOBA Show.

do so, and now he will take him into the show ring. I'm with them in spirit, however. When Don comes home, he's so excited. Apollo 18 had taken 2nd place and won a red ribbon. The judge commented that Apollo's fleece had not quite developed yet; he was only 8 months old. But next year, look out! we expect him to really come into his own.

March 13, 2011

I receive a number of calls and e-mails from Michelle. She has been out of town on business all last week. Today she brings us a homemade chicken noodle cas-

serole. *How very kind of her! And the food is absolutely delicious. It so helps Don with meal preparation. Thank you, Michelle.*

March 16, 2011

I have an appointment with Dr. Diamond and look forward to seeing him again. After all, he had been my doctor for over seven years. He thinks I'm doing fine, but adds a few more blood tests for my next blood draw and gives me an appointment in six months. My main doctor is now Dr. Yang and the medical personnel at Transplant Services. I miss seeing Dr. Diamond as much as I had in the past.

March 29, 2011

I see the endocrinologist again, and at this visit, he decreases my finger sticks to twice a day for blood sugar checks and decreases my medicine to just one-half a pill every morning. I'm very happy to oblige.

April 2, 2011

Time to look again at my incisions. Ah, they're healing well. The incisions that were made to place and later remove the PD catheter have closed nicely. The incision to put my new kidney into my abdominal cavity is also healing well and gradually becoming paler. The surgeons did not remove my old kidneys, as that procedure is quite invasive. Sometimes it's done if a patient has high, uncontrollable blood pressures, but mine are not. My old kidneys which are above my waist in the back are no longer functioning. My new kidney rests in the front lower right-hand section of my abdomen.

Tonight, I take my first bath in six months. It feels so-o good to be able to lie down in very warm water and just relax. I had almost gotten used to taking showers, but it never stopped me from looking forward to my first bath with my new kidney. One of life's simple pleasures has just returned.

June 7, 2011

I see my endocrinologist today and he tells me he is discharging me. My A1C blood test (an important marker for monitoring diabetes) has come back with good results. My "temporary" diabetes is gone. Such wonderful news. I'm elated! No more fingersticks and no more watching my diet so closely. My prednisone dose is now 2.5 mg on Monday, Wednesday, and Friday, and 5 mg the rest of the week. I'm certain the drop in dosage has helped my "temporary" diabetes. **God is so good to me! Thank you, Lord.**

The staff at the endocrinologist's office give me hugs as they say goodbye. They are so happy to see me doing so well. We reminisce when I first came to their office, wearing a mask and really quite ill. I certainly have come a long way.

To be on an unrestricted diet is such a plus. No more weighing food. No more counting calories. I can eat anything and everything I want, and I'm simply thrilled. I do need to watch portions, so as not to gain any unneeded weight. I love food and have always enjoyed cooking and baking. To be unlimited in what I can eat was more than I had ever bargained for, as I have been on so many restricted diets during the past six years.

June 13, 2011

Today, I have an appointment with my hematologist.

When I was discharged from the hospital, my hemoglobin was 9.2 g. This was due to kidney failure and not to any blood loss during surgery. I was told I lost about a whiskey glass full of blood during surgery, very little. My new kidney seemed to kick in right away, producing the hormone that enabled the bone marrow to make the red blood cells, and my H&H increased to 10.2 g, 32%. But then my H&H stayed at that number for about two months and did not increase. I began having problems with shortness of breath.

*It was thought that another injection of Aranesp from the hematologist was necessary, just to help the kidney get started again. Transplant Services made an appointment for me, and it was in two weeks. During that time, my kidney must have begun working again because when I arrived at the doctor's office, he asked me, "Why did you come?" I told him, and he turned the computer screen around and showed me my current H&H results. They were now 11.6 g and 36.7%. Just all so miraculous to me. I am no longer anemic! **Thank you, dear God.***

I still have the hot flashes and night sweats. It was thought that the cause may be my medications, but since I had this before my surgery, I believe it's hormonal. I can put up with it, however, no problem. I just concentrate on all my other health improvements, and I am so happy.

It's amazing to me just how much, and what, I as a patient have forgotten with time. Time seems to have erased many of the difficulties, discomforts, and anxieties of my hospitalization and recuperative period. If it wasn't for writing this book, all that would have become hazy to me by now. I am so engrossed in the positive things that are happening all around me that the formidable times are no longer a very real memory.

Strange, too, now that I look back on my recovery period, how very much in the moment I lived, minute by minute. Then, I was aware of only myself and my immediate surroundings. It was a very peaceful time, a most reflective time. I never betrayed the moment. My life has now returned to a "normal" pace, busy and way too stressful. I can only remember that slow, quiet recovery period with a smile and an appreciation of what it truly was.

CHAPTER 16

Don Shares

I OFTEN WONDERED WHAT my husband was actually thinking as I was going through my illness stages and hospitalization. I really wanted to know. One of the hardest conversations I ever had with Don was when we sat down together and began to talk about this. He is not a very emotional man and it was really not an easy subject to approach with him.

First, let me give you some background on my husband. We have been married for almost 29 years, and we're usually always seen together, although we have some very different interests. We work as partners in our businesses as well. Don is rather laid back and always seems in control. A very solid man. He is a good man, a caring man, a dependable man, and a very hard worker. His sense of humor sort of sneaks up on me and he often makes me laugh. We can be talking about something seriously, and then all of a sudden, he

Don and Carole cutting their 25th
Wedding Anniversary cake.

throws in a curve, a funny comment. What I admire
most about him though is his loyalty to his country.
Don is extremely patriotic and quite knowledgeable
about American history, the United States military, and
politics. A large American flag proudly hangs on our
front porch.

I am a fairly independent woman, so I tried not to
lean too heavily on Don during my illness, although
relying on him was very easy. When things became

130

really difficult, however, I knew he would be there for me. And he always was.

Don was born on a dairy farm in York Springs, PA, the oldest of three children. Perhaps because he worked so hard on the farm, he developed one of the strongest work ethics I've ever known any man to have. Following high school, he attended DeVry Institute in Chicago and graduated as an electrical engineer. He had an interesting career path. Don worked for the aerospace industry and provided tracking station support for satellites launched by the Air Force and Navy. That was before I met him. When our paths first crossed in the 1980s, he was a computer programming consultant for software project management on large-scale computer systems. Don is a very intelligent man and has an excellent memory. I wish my memory was as good.

Don went with me to all my support meetings and attended most of my dialysis classes. He accompanied me to many of my doctor appointments as well, especially as I became less functional. Shortly before dialysis, Don said, "I could see Carole's health deteriorating. It was very frustrating for me because there seemed so little I could do. But I didn't expect her deterioration to happen so fast. From September to December 2010, she went downhill quickly." He said my skin became a yellow/grey color as the toxins built up in my body. Even though I tried using a little more makeup, it seemed no amount of makeup could rid me of this sickly look.

I asked Don what he thought when the first shipment of dialysis supplies arrived. "I was just shocked! The driver of the truck unloaded a skid and a half of boxes containing solutions and supplies on the driveway, all shrink-wrapped. I was concerned about the weight of these boxes and where to place them in our bedroom to prevent the floorboards from bowing. It was a challenge."

"I wasn't sure how long Carole would be on dialysis — six months, six years? But then, none of us really knew. I just had to take one day at a time. That was all I could do."

The listings on the National Kidney Transplant List and the Paired Donor List were an emotional roller coaster. "I wanted to see Carole through this, but I felt so helpless. I prayed for God to guide me through this."

Don did not expect Jay to step forward as a donor. "It was such a shock! Now, I understand the impact Carole really had on her life. It takes a very special person to make the decision to donate a kidney."

"When I heard Carole needed a transplant, I was afraid and unsure how to best support her. I was unable to give her my kidney because I have hypertension. On the morning of her surgery, I felt at peace that God would see us through this hospital stay. Everything moved so quickly that morning. I waited for five hours before they would even let me in the RR. I saw Carole with a towel over her head, and she acknowledged me, but she was really drugged and out of it."

"I was surprised how very pink, almost red, her urine was," Don said. "I saw that, but since it didn't seem to bother the doctors, I decided I wouldn't let it bother me." He said he pushed my IV pole as I was wheeled to ICU and stayed with me until about 9 p.m. that first evening. Finally, after some reassurance from the ICU nurse, he went home. Don said he prayed for me "many times."

Following discharge, Don was very concerned about keeping me safe from an infection. He took such good care of me; in fact, he doted on me. He was there and met my every need. He did all the cooking for me and made sure I had three good meals a day to eat. Every seven days, he helped me fill my pill box, which was quite a chore. It took some time to do because my pills were many and some had to be cut in half. "I was simply overwhelmed, and I didn't even have to take them!" Don commented.

Once home, he said, "It seemed to take awhile before I noticed any improvement, but once Carole turned the corner, it became more evident. The recovery process was unsettling — I could only take it one day at a time again, some days just one hour at a time. This whole situation, to see this all unfold, strengthened my faith in God. Until you have actually witnessed a miracle, you don't really know... Carole's recovery process is the only miracle I have ever seen with my own eyes."

Don kept our embroidery and monogramming business going throughout my poor health, the surgery and the entire healing process. I don't know exactly how he did it, but those of you who own your own business know that sometimes this is exactly what you must do. More than for financial reasons, it's that people and businesses are dependent on you and you cannot let them down.

Don took six months off from his flying lessons to be with me constantly and only returned to class when

Carole shows some of her embroidered kitchen /
guest towels in *Amazing Monograms*.

he felt confident that I would be okay. "I am so pleased
with the end result," he said. "A new kidney has given
her a second lease on life. We're looking forward now,
never again looking back in that rear-view mirror. And
life is looking so good!"

CHAPTER 17

Meeting My Donor

Winston Churchill once said, "We make a living by what we get. We make a life by what we give." Surely my donor must have known that.

Some may think, "Why would someone even want to donate their kidney? Do they realize what they're doing?" Research reveals that over 92% of living donors had no regrets about donating, were very satisfied with their transplant experience, and would make the same decision to donate again today. There are many reasons for a live donor wanting to donate their kidney, the main one being to help improve the health of someone they know. Choosing to donate a kidney and give the gift of life is one of the most meaningful things anyone can do.

Confidentiality had always been stressed to us, so I thought that getting a donor's phone number was next to impossible. However, I also believed that talking with a live donor versus with the family of a deceased donor were two different scenarios, so I decided to risk it and simply ask. I was told then the name of my kidney donor was Marlane Parrotta and she was from Pittsburgh. Yes! Apparently, Marlane wanted to talk to me as much as I wanted to talk to her, so she approved the giving of her phone number to me. Wow! Jay and Marlane — two ordinary people doing something extraordinary.

At the time I was given Marlane's phone number, I still had voice problems, so I decided to wait another week or two before actually making the call. I hoped I would really connect with her, but who knows? Maybe we wouldn't even like each other. It was a suspenseful time, a time when I imagined all kinds of initial conversations.

March 18, 2011

I just can't wait any longer! I dial her number at 9:30 a.m. today and leave a message on her answering machine, along with my phone number, but I also say that I will call again this evening. At 12:30 p.m., she calls me back, and oh, my! what an emotional phone call it is! "Are you the lady that has my kidney?" she asks. "Yes, that's me! That's me!" I exclaim. And we both just laugh and laugh. I love her laugh, and she just seems so nice.

We immediately connect. It's very easy to talk to Marlane, like we have been friends forever. We share our stories. I tell her about Jay, and she tells me about Regina (Reggie) Risher, her friend and the other kidney recipient. I thank her profusely, and she comments that it was such a good experience for her, that it was her joy. We talk about meeting some day, whenever everyone is well enough to travel. Perhaps we can find a halfway point between here and Pittsburgh to meet.

Marlane said she is doing just fine. She was nauseated from the anesthesia following surgery, but anesthesia usually bothers her. Her friend, Reggie, who received Jay's kidney, is having a difficult time. She is a diabetic and apparently has had some stomach problems with the medication. They altered her medication dose a bit, and she said she's feeling a little better. I'm so sorry to hear this, but hope that with time, the problem will resolve for her.

Marlane and I exchange e-mail addresses, as we hope to stay in contact this way. She doesn't have a computer, but one of her three sons lives nearby, and she plans to use his. That'll work.

Well, this is just like the icing on the cake — to know who donated your new kidney to you and to be able to thank her. It just doesn't get any better than that. I so look forward to the day when we can meet and I can thank her personally.

When I asked Marlane what this experience meant to her, this was her response:

"For me, this was one of the easiest decisions I had ever made. I knew a security guard in the building where I worked, and he was on dialysis for quite awhile. He received a kidney, and when he returned to work, I was looking at a new man! Then Reggie, a co-worker of mine for almost six years, told me she was on the National Kidney Transplant List, but she knew that a living donor would be her best chance. This was an opportunity for me to do something that would make a tremendous difference in her life...and what a privilege it was for me. Unfortunately, though, we were not a match.

"It was then suggested that we be placed on the Kidney Paired Donor List. We were given two chances to match, but each one was not meant to be. I always believed that God had a plan for us, and that in His wisdom, He saw the bigger picture. And as they say, 'The third time's the charm,' and we had a match. In the end, God did have a most excellent plan for us, and I count it a blessing to have been a part of it all!"

I asked Jay the same question, and she answered:

"This was a life-changing experience for me, and it has taught me that miracles do happen.

"Anything is possible if you are willing to believe that it will happen. Life is such a blessing. We don't always appreciate it until something goes wrong. We should all treasure our life daily, and when possible, take the time to help others. Carole and I are now doing great, and I am so thankful for the opportunity I had to give her a second chance at a normal life."

Reggie responded this way:

"The Kidney Paired Donor List was a true miracle. When I was told by a friend that she would give me her kidney, I thought she was joking. When she assured me she was willing to be a donor, I was stunned! What a great example of Christianity! Then her testing began, and we found out we were not a match. That was a difficult day. We were entered into a computer system and wow, they found two other matches. So we went from two people in renal failure to two people with functioning kidneys. Now that is a true miracle!"

I had been told that sometimes the organ recipient experiences the characteristics of the organ donor. I found this intriguing. I remembered speaking with a man at a support meeting last year who told Don and me about his recuperative period following his kidney transplant. He became very interested in the cooking shows on TV, so much so that he soon became familiar with the names of all the TV chefs and knew their personalities. He began jotting down some of their recipes, too, and trying them in the kitchen. He realized he really loved to cook! Prior to his surgery, he could barely boil water. Now his wife takes a back seat and he is the family cook. Later, he learned that his donor was quite an experienced cook, not a trained chef, but one who could always be found in the kitchen, trying new recipes and cooking away.

Another example of this was a pilot friend of Don's who passed away of a cerebral aneurysm. His wife signed the papers to donate all his organs, and his liver went to a man in Pennsylvania. This recipient wrote many letters to her expressing his deep gratitude for her husband's liver. In one letter he asked if her husband was especially fond of coffee. The recipient never liked coffee before, but now he had become a "coffeeholic." The wife wrote back, "A pilot? Are you kidding? Absolutely! He lived on coffee, nonstop!"

I'm still waiting for a characteristic of Marlane's to occur within me. I would be honored. So far, though, I haven't really noticed anything different about me. Perhaps with time.

Since my surgery, a few people have asked me, "How do you feel living with another person's kidney inside you?" Now, I must admit, I am rarely at a loss for words, but the first time I heard this question, I was just shocked. I thought it was an awful question to ask. In fact, I had never really thought about it until I was asked. I have decided that in the future, I would just reply, "Wonderful! Absolutely wonderful!" Since given the gift of life, this is the only way I would want to answer such an absurd question.

Sunday, June 5, 2011

I am so looking forward to today…ever since we decided this was the day we would all meet for our first reunion. By all, I mean my kidney donor, Marlane; her friend, Reggie and her husband, Doug; Jay, who gave her kidney to Reggie; and Don and me. What a joyous day this is going to be! Don and I drive out to Bedford, PA, from Mechanicsburg, a halfway point for both groups to meet, and Marlane, Reggie, Doug, and Jay come in from Pittsburgh. So at 11:30 a.m., right in front of Ed's Steakhouse, we have our first joyous gathering. We meet each other with lots of hugs and smiles and "How are you doing?" I am so excited and happy! It just doesn't get any better than this. Strangers bonded by generosity, the progress of medicine, and by God's great plan.

We sit down in a relatively small room in the back of the restaurant, which we have mostly to ourselves, and the conversations begin. We are so anxious to share our medical journeys and compare notes. Such fun! The recipients thank their donors over and over again for they have made the recipients' current good health possible. And we all did look the picture of good health! We talk about making this an annual event, and I'm sure we will. I invite Marlane to visit Don and me in Mechanicsburg, so I could show her my little corner of the world, and she says she would love to come. It's a day that exceeds all expectations. I'm smiling constantly...and it all starts from within my heart.

Jay continued to look for work. She was also looking for a career change. Don encouraged her to include in her resume the fact that she was a recent kidney donor. He felt this was very revealing of her character. So Jay did. Recently, she went on an interview at a large dental office in the Pittsburgh area. The dentist interviewing her noticed the date she had donated her kidney. It rang a bell. He asked Jay if she knew Reggie and Marlane, two other workers in his office, and of course, Jay did. She got

Our first meeting in Bedford — a picture of health!
Left to right: Jay, kidney donor; Reggie, Jay's
kidney recipient; Marlane, kidney donor;
Carole, Marlane's kidney recipient.

Carole and Jay at the Bedford meeting.

the job and is so enjoying this new career change. What an amazing coincidence, truly amazing! It reminded me of just how small the world really is. And what catalysts for change kidney transplants have become.

I recently learned that Jay is pregnant and is due to have her baby in spring. Don and I are so excited for this young couple. We hope a bright and happy future lies ahead for all of them.

Epilogue

LIFE AFTER TRANSPLANT has been a continuous education for both Don and me. There are ongoing challenges for us, as well as the transplant professionals. The goal now is to exchange information, allowing me to develop some coping skills, perhaps change a few behaviors, and focus on wellness. The first six months post-op is sometimes considered a "picture window" of the future for a transplant patient. My recovery period has gone very smoothly. It has truly been a miracle. And I believe it's totally because of the power of prayer.

In September 2011, because I'm in the drug research program, a routine kidney biopsy was ordered. Truth be told, I was more concerned about the procedure than the results. A biopsy provides a microscopic look into the deep tissues of the new kidney. The actual procedure, however, went very well and took only about 15 minutes. Initially, an ultrasound is done to locate the new kidney, and then tiny segments are removed for analysis. When it was determined that the kidney wasn't bleeding, I was discharged. One week later, I received the biopsy report. I had passed with flying colors. It revealed "no acute infections and no acute rejection," and I was ecstatic.

Everyone I see comments on how well I look and I just smile happily. I have been transplanted to better health, indeed. I know that not all outcomes are as positive as mine. By the grace of God only have I come through this so well and often wonder why God has been so very good to me. I'm in total thanksgiving for the outpouring of support from my family, friends, and churches. It makes my heart sing.

Life goes on and I am feeling absolutely wonderful. I sleep so well at night — no sound of the cycler and no lights, tubes, or bags. I am a free woman and it's a great feeling. My coloring is so good, no yellow/grey skin. My energy level is way up and I can easily get through a busy day. I used to sleep ten hours a day plus naps, and now I need only 7 or 8 hours of sleep each night. More hours to live my life, and more hours to live it more fully. My quality of life has improved by levels I had never dreamt possible. My diet is totally unrestricted. I can eat anything, and believe me, I do. Probably only another kidney patient could truly understand this joy.

No one is guaranteed tomorrow, least of all me. I'm so thankful for this transplant, but I realize my body can reject this new kidney on any day, at any given time, and even without symptoms. I'm willing to take that chance. I place this thought in the back of my mind and try to live each day without concentrating on what can happen.

In a recent e-mail, Marlane said,

"So glad to hear you are doing so well! I truly wish and pray that more people would consider donating. It hasn't affected me physically at all, and if people would understand that, maybe they wouldn't be so reluctant to donate. Just knowing that someone else's life could change so dramatically..."

She said it all.

I believe in the power of storytelling, and I hope her comments in particular and my story in general will encourage those who may be considering organ donation to do so. While living donation is not for everyone, it can be the closest thing to a miracle that anyone will ever experience.

Well, this has been my journey and my journey alone. Every kidney patient has a story to tell about his/her own journey, and no two are alike. I encourage you to write down your journey. The full impact of what you've been through will become more vivid for you, taking on a life of its own.

It is my hope that my story will help others by creating a big picture of kidney disease — the struggles, the heartaches, the joys, and the successes. Despite the discouraging times, please be encouraged that there are really good times ahead. Never give up. God will be there for you, seeing you through the dark days until your life goes on, better than ever before. Believe this, and you, too, or your family member or friend will be transplanted to better health.

Fifteen Facts About Organ Donation and Transplantation

There are currently over 100,000 people waiting for transplant in this country. The success rates of transplant surgery have improved remarkably, but growing shortages exist in the supply of organs and tissues available for transplantation. Many Americans who need transplants cannot get them because of these shortages. The result: some of these people die while waiting for that "Gift of Life."

Each year, the National Kidney Foundation develops special public education programs aimed at increasing public awareness of the need for organ and tissue donation. Learning more about organ and tissue donation will help every American to make an informed decision about this important issue. Here are some facts everyone should know:

1. In the U.S., 104,748 patients are currently waiting for an organ transplant; more than 4,000 new patients are added to the waiting list each month.

2. Every day, 18 people die while waiting for a transplant of a vital organ, such as a heart, liver, kidney, pancreas, lung, or bone marrow.

3. Because of the lack of available donors in this country, 4,573 kidney patients, 1,506 liver patients, 371 heart patients, and 234 lung patients died in 2008 while waiting for life-saving organ transplants.

4. Nearly 10 percent of the patients currently waiting for heart transplants are young people under 18. Acceptable organ donors can range in age from newborn to 65 years or more. People who are 65 years of age or older may be acceptable donors, particularly of corneas, skin, and bone, and for total body donation.

5. An estimated 12,000 people who die each year meet the criteria for organ donation, but fewer than half of that number actually became organ donors.

6. Donor organs are matched to waiting recipients by a national computer registry called the National Organ Procurement and Transplantation Network (OPTN). This computer registry is operated by an organization known as the United Network for Organ Sharing (UNOS), which is located in Richmond, Virginia.

7. Currently there are 58 organ procurement organizations (OPOs) across the country, which provide organ procurement services to 250 transplant centers.

8. All hospitals are required by law to have a "Required Referral" system in place. Under this system, the hospital must notify the local OPO

of all patient deaths. If the OPO determines that organ and/or tissue donation is appropriate in a particular case, they will have a representative contact the deceased patient's family to offer them the option of donating their loved one's organs and tissues.

9. By signing a Uniform Donor Card, an individual indicates his or her wish to be a donor. However, at the time of death, the person's next of kin will still be asked to sign a consent form for donation. It is important for people who wish to be organ and tissue donors to tell their family about this decision so that their wishes will be honored at the time of death.

10. All costs related to the donation of organs and tissues are paid for by the donor program. A family who receives a bill by mistake should contact the hospital or procurement agency immediately.

11. Advances in surgical technique and organ preservation and the development of more effective drugs to prevent rejection have improved the success rates of all types of organ and tissue transplants.

12. About 94.4 percent of the kidneys transplanted from cadavers are still functioning well at one year after surgery.

13. The results are even better for kidneys transplanted from living donors. One year after surgery, 97.96 percent of these kidneys were still functioning well.

14. Following are one-year patient and organ graft survival rates:

Organ	Patient Survival Rate	Graft Survival Rate
Kidney (cadaveric)	94.4%	89.0%
Kidney (live donor)	97.9%	95.1%
Liver	90.1%	82.0%

15. Following is a comparison of the numbers of organ transplants done in 2008 and the numbers of individuals who are on the national waiting list as of November 2009.

Organ	Transplants in 2008	Patients on Waiting List
Kidney	16,520	82,364
Kidney / Pancreas	837	2,220
Pancreas	436	1,488
Liver	6,319	15,915
Heart	2,163	2,884
Heart / Lung	27	83
Lung	1,478	1,863
Intestine	185	229
Total	27,965	107,046

Source: http://www.kidney.org
© 2011 National Kidney Foundation, Inc. Used by permission.

Resources

www.kfcp.org — The Kidney Foundation of Central Pennsylvania is dedicated to providing health education and screening for chronic kidney disease, services and support to people whose lives are impacted by kidney disease, and advocacy for living organ donation in order to reduce the wait for a life-saving kidney transplant. For more information about the Patient and Family Partner Program, or any services for people with kidney disease, contact KFCP at 1-800-762-6202 or by e-mail at info@kfcp.org.

www.kidney.org — The National Kidney Foundation is a health organization focused on the prevention of kidney disease and the improvement of the health of anyone affected by the disease. This website includes personal stories, definitions of medical terminology, legislation relevant to donation, recipient message boards, and e-mail discussion groups.

www.donors1.org — Founded in 1974, the Gift of Life Donor Program is the nonprofit organ and tissue donor program serving the eastern half of PA, southern NJ, and DE. The program offers numerous educational programs designed to increase public awareness of and commitment to organ and tissue donation. 1-800-DONORS-1.

www.unos.org — The United Network for Organ Sharing (UNOS) is the nonprofit organization responsible for maintaining the nation's organ transplant waiting list for organs from people who have died. In addition to information about the waiting list, the "Transplant Living" section of the website has updated statistics on living donation, information about the transplant process, and information about financing transplantation.

www.helpHOPElive.org — HelpHOPELive is the place to fundraise for anyone dealing with the many challenges related to a transplant or catastrophic injury. They provide the consultation needed to raise funds to bridge the gap between what health insurance will pay and what is actually needed to heal, live and thrive. Call 1-800-642-8399 or get started right now with their online application (www.helphopelive.org/online-application).

www.transweb.org — TransWeb is a nonprofit organ donation and transplantation educational website that includes donor and recipient stories, medical literature about donation, and information on the different surgical procedures.

Acknowledgements

I AM NOT A WRITER, by nature or training, but it has been my heartfelt wish to reach out with compassion and encouragement to kidney patients. I want to help them on their journey by simply telling them what has happened to me on mine. Few patients have accomplished this by writing a book.

A special thank you to Carolyn Kimmel, herself a writer, who took my raw manuscript filled with four years of journal entries and suggested I turn them into chapters and thereby tell my story. Thus began the first of many, many rewrites. Without her insight and encouragement, this book would never read as it does today. Perhaps it wouldn't even have happened.

A special thank you to Nasrollah Ghahramani, MD, MS, FACP, a nephrologist at the Departments of Medicine and Public Health Sciences of Penn State Hershey College of Medicine, who provided assistance with the review and medical editing of this book. His kindness in supporting me with my limited medical knowledge was noted and appreciated.

There are not enough words to thank Patti Bucek, executive director of the Kidney Foundation of Central PA, for her guidance and support. She was there for me from the very beginning and in the end offered her endorsement of this book.

I owe biggest love and thanks to Steve Hoy and Leslie Hoy of *Church Road Books*, who literally took my manuscript through its final stages. I am forever grateful for Steve's knowledge and expertise in crafting this book to print. Our countless back-and-forth e-mails exhausted many of my days, as decision after decision was made. I will miss these e-mails. His suggestions were numerous and always worthy of my following.

Leslie Hoy is truly a gifted editor and proofreader. Her way with words is something I can only dream of possessing. Her command of the English language and grammar rules boggles my mind, and I'm envious of what comes to her so naturally.

Finally, a special thank you to my husband, whose patience with my use of our main computer for many hours daily was beyond his tolerance level, but he endured it anyway. His support and love were endless.

My deepest thanks and love to the many people who are part of this book through their e-mails and kind thoughts. You know who you are.

You have all contributed not only to this book...but to my life. May God bless you.

"Thy will be done..." And it was so.

Made in the USA
Charleston, SC
20 September 2012